Also by David Bertolacci:

Tree People of Tepui, a children's guide to discovery. Hyla, a young apprentice, learns about what his people know of their universe, the tree, and questions how they came to be.

See <u>GrandSlamTheory.com</u> for more information.

GRAND SLAM THEORY OF THE OMNIVERSE

What Happened before the Big Bang?

DAVID BERTOLACCI

BALBOA.
PRESS

A DIVISION OF HAY HOUSE

Balboa Press books may be ordered through booksellers or by contacting:

Balboa Press
A Division of Hay House
1663 Liberty Drive
Bloomington, IN 47403
www.balboapress.com
1 (877) 407-4847

Because of the dynamic nature of the Internet, any web addresses or links contained in
this book may have changed since publication and may no longer be valid. The views
expressed in this work are solely those of the author and do not necessarily reflect the
views of the publisher, and the publisher hereby disclaims any responsibility for them.

The author of this book does not dispense medical advice or prescribe the use
of any technique as a form of treatment for physical, emotional, or medical
problems without the advice of a physician, either directly or indirectly. The
intent of the author is only to offer information of a general nature to help you
in your quest for emotional and spiritual well-being. In the event you use any
of the information in this book for yourself, which is your constitutional right,
the author and the publisher assume no responsibility for your actions.

Any people depicted in stock imagery provided by Thinkstock are models,
and such images are being used for illustrative purposes only.
Certain stock imagery © Thinkstock.

Printed in the United States of America.

ISBN: 978-1-4525-8419-5 (sc)
ISBN: 978-1-4525-8421-8 (hc)
ISBN: 978-1-4525-8420-1 (e)

Library of Congress Control Number: 2013918205

Balboa Press rev. date: 08/18/2014

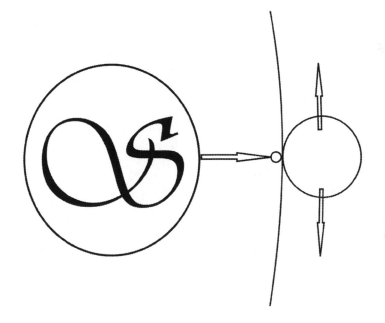

For Crystal
Thank you for being my inspiration.

"As a lotus flower is born in water, grows in water
and rises out of water to stand above it unsoiled,
so I, born in the world, raised in the world having overcome the world,
live unsoiled by the world.
–*Hindu Prince Gautama Siddhartha (The Buddha)*

TABLE OF CONTENTS

ILLUSTRATIONS

ACRONYMS USED

AMS — Alpha Magnetic Spectrometer
CCC — conformal cyclic cosmology
CMB — cosmic microwave background
CME — coronal mass ejection
COBE — Cosmic Background Explorer
EM — Electromagnetic
EPR — Einstein, Podolsky, and Rosen
GUT — Grand Unified Theory
LHC — Large Hadron Collider
QFT — Quantum Field Theory
QCD — Quantum Chromodynamics
QED — Quantum Electrodynamics
SM — Standard Model
TeV — teraelectronvolt
WIMP — Weakly Interacting Massive Particle
WMAP — Wilkinson Microwave Anisotropy Probe

PREFACE

Are you curious about where the universe came from? Like many before me, I always wondered how the universe began. Even when I was a child in Sunday School, I asked: If God created the universe, then who created God? In science class I learned about outer space. Again, I asked questions that seemed to be different from what was just accepted, or assumed to be correct. Was space really empty? To me, space has always contained *everything*. What we think of as empty is just swimming with things we have not discovered yet. We are at the dawn of a new age in science when we are finally discovering that space is actually full of energy. I refer to the new age as our *"Independence Age"* of science, named after two new discoveries discussed in this book that were both announced on Independence Day 2012.

I have studied science my whole life to attempt to answer my own questions about our place in the universe and how we came to be. In the 20th century, modern science has provided many answers and a brilliant model of how the universe began. The scientific explanation miraculously mirrors the ancient religious writings for the creation of the universe. Our modern explanation of creation is known as the *Big Bang Theory*. According to the Big Bang Theory, a single particle the size of a tiny point – a singularity consisting of all of the universe's energy – expanded because according to the laws of physics as we know them, it was not stable. The resulting rapid inflation began a series of reactions and nearly infinite expansion as energies, forces, subatomic particles, and what we know today as matter were formed.

This book does not argue how the events of the Big Bang unfolded out into the universe as we know it today. Rather, it delves into the question of how the singularity came to exist in the first place. By assuming that time starts when the Big Bang starts and cutting out anything that happened *before* the Big Bang, modern science may be looking at only a small part of a bigger picture. Moreover, just considering part of the process may be what has led us to an incomplete understanding of our universe today. Our universe consists of forces and matter which comprise less than 5% of the total energies that have been calculated.

A problem that exists in today's models includes a lack of an explanation of the true nature of gravity that, as we know it, is far weaker than the other forces, such as electromagnetism, weak, and strong nuclear forces. Dark matter was proposed as an answer to the observations that our galaxy's mass was imbalanced. Dark matter can be observed by indirect effect, but nobody knows what it is. Another enigma about our current universe is the infinite expansion of our cosmos, which was previously thought to eventually collapse inward due to gravity. Dark energy was proposed when it was discovered that the universe as a whole is not only expanding but also accelerating. Objects in the distant universe move away from us at a faster pace the farther they are from us. Many attempts have been made to explain Dark energy, but it remains an unknown.

This book presents the ideological concept of the *Omniverse*, which is a model based on a simple principle of known laws of physics that expands on the idea of the Big Bang. I had initially realized that we only have a small part of the entire process. As crazy as it sounds, an individual came to me in a dream after I set the intention to learn all that is to know about the universe. The concept was stored in my subconscious until my "ah-ha" moment when I realized a system in motion, or a simple energy transfer, describes the Omniverse in a simple, efficient manner. In the mid-90s, I saw a popular physicist on TV saying that someday someone would come up with an equation an inch long that describes everything in the universe, and this inspired me to search for it.

My background is in geology with an emphasis on mineralogy and geochemistry, so finding an equation out of all that we know about physics seems like a daunting task. I admit that I was not the best student in calculus, but my education included healthy amounts of chemistry and physics because geology is basically an applied science that combines all others. This is why I am presenting the Omniverse model as a graphic representation and asking the scientific community to look at it in whole or in parts, to apply mathematical principles, find hypotheses to test and observe effects, and ultimately formulate a theory utilizing this proposal as a jump-start to the entire process. This book presents a summary of the most successful theories of physics and discoveries of today, the proposal of the Omniverse model, and a comparison to how current theories might work within the framework of the Omniverse model.

This book is not intended to be a replacement for any theories explaining the Big Bang series of events, but it can be used to supplement the information. It is also not intended to be an argument of science versus religion, which I believe are basically different versions used to explain the same phenomena. This book is not a peer-reviewed document, but it is intended to be written for everybody who is interested in the subject. I am granting readers of this book full permission to use the principles proposed herein in the hopes of advancing not only our current understanding of the universe, but also expanding our very ideas of where we, as humans, fit into the puzzle.

The reader should ultimately question everything that we know about creation and evolution. It is not, and will never be, a closed book because we will always be learning in further detail how we came to be and striving to define what our role is in the universe. It is my personal belief that knowledge gained from reading this book will help people with the process of understanding what a universal consciousness means and how to feel as one with the universe. However, these topics are from personal gain and whether or not a reader gains insight is up to each and every individual.

ACKNOWLEDGEMENTS

The author would like to thank so many people for helping materialize the creation of this book from just a thought in the mind's eye. My wife, Crystal Bertolacci, has been absolutely instrumental in the process of writing this book. Mark Basoco, the editor of this book, helped put the project together. So many other people along the way have given me inspiration, and they are too many to list.

During a long period of researching, I have become involved with other spiritually-minded people, and I give special thanks to all. It was a total surprise that following a path of logic and science would also bring me down a spiritual path. Special thanks to all of the ancients who realized the importance of documenting and teaching their ideas with the intent of teaching across all generations. I would also like to thank the Art of Living and founder Sri Sri Ravi Shankar, because it was their meditation techniques that helped clear the mind to begin writing.

There have been so many signs telling me to write this book, it was as if the universe itself was telling me to write so it could learn about its own nature. For this, I thank the universe and its messengers, the Angels for showing the way of my path. This project has been just as much about my personal discoveries as the advances in science that have taken place to help describe the Omniverse. This project marks a new beginning for the understanding of the nature of the universe. Finally, thank *you* for reading this book! You are the most important part of the process. You are the reason I have undertaken this journey. When your children ask you where the universe came from, you will have the answer!

PART

1

INTRODUCTION

"Love is not just an emotion. It is your very existence."
—*Sri Sri Ravi Shankar*

It was a hot and humid summer day in Chicago, unusually hot for the windy city known for its especially bitter cold winters. It felt like a sweltering heat; the kind where you could just melt right into the asphalt. The smells of hot dogs, burgers and sausages on grills everywhere permeated the thick, hot air creating what feels like an unquenchable thirst. Only a slight breeze blew over the cars in the parking lots and crowds of people who kept gathering regardless of the summer heat. There were families playing ball in the parking lot, groups of people tailgating, and crowds trying to get into the stadium to see tonight's big game. Many were diehard fans that were there for every game, every season. Some were there for their first time, to experience the magic as never seen before. But no one knew what would ensue on this magical night.

On this day, the gathering fans were at Wrigley Field listening to the crowd roar while enjoying freshly grilled hot dogs and cold beer, waiting for that special moment to begin. Play ball! Later in the night, the moment heated up with a tie game. It was a real nail-biter. Then, deep in the ninth inning with the bases loaded, the crowd lulled to a quiet hush as the pitcher wound up. After so many hits, game after game, this was the moment everyone had all been waiting for with the star hitter at the plate.

With the bases loaded, everyone in the crowd on the home team's side wants to see our star batter hit a home run, of course. The pitcher goes through his ritual. He holds the ball in his glove and peers out of the corner of his eyes to scan where everybody is in the infield and outfield. He winds up and gets ready to deliver his pitch. He wants to send that ball right down the middle, a fastball too fast for the batter to even see. But the batter knew exactly what was coming.

Suddenly, the crack of the ball being struck is heard by everyone as clear as day, as if it were right next to each and every person in the stands. The crowd reacts as if in slow motion, watching the baseball fly upwards in the sky. Everyone gets up out of their seats, forgetting about the nachos in their lap with only the ball on their mind, still going upwards. The crowd roars louder as the ball keeps sailing until it goes right out of the park! This is the moment we have been waiting for.

Any baseball hit within the park can become a single, double, triple, home run, or just a fly ball. It took a pitch just right and a perfect swing. The ball went flying toward the outfield with enough momentum to become a *grand slam,* and all of the players came running home. Victory is sealed as the crowd goes absolutely crazy with fans jumping from their seats, losing their food and drinks that were instantly forgotten in the sight of the ball that was still flying upward in the sky. On this magical night, that ball had so much momentum behind it that it never stopped and just flew right out of the stadium, into the parking lot where many tailgating fans had been waiting. This was truly a special moment and a very rare occasion, but the dedicated fans who waited outside the stadium knew that it would happen eventually, and if they waited long enough and came to every game, it could happen again. This baseball was no ordinary baseball, but a grand slam that was hit hard enough to clear the stands to sail free of the confines of the park. And so many special fans were there to observe this grand slam, which became a monumental victory for the home team!

After being knocked out of the park, this grand slam became a legend that no one would forget. For years to come, athletes, announcers, and fans alike would remember this very moment and talk about it as if it were the defining moment of their lives. Writers would compare every other victory in the game to this one because it was that special. Even the ball, which at one time was just like any other ordinary baseball, becomes much more valuable. Can you imagine finding such a rare gem at an online auction after passing from fan to fan, gaining value? Can you imagine how much it is worth now? This ball is not just an ordinary baseball.

On an astronomical level, this is similar to the great feat leading to the moment that sparked the creation, forming our own universe. And we are the fans at the ball park who observed it for the first time. As our lives go on, we are the ones who discuss how great this was and how it created what our lives have become today. Many books have been written about what happened after this moment, called the *Big Bang*. But we remember what happened inside the stadium, when it was a Grand Slam!

According to the Big Bang theory[1] a single particle the size of a tiny point that consisted of all of the universe's energies expanded because, according to known laws of physics, it could not be stable existing as the single particle. The resulting rapid inflation began a series of reactions and infinite expansion as energies, forces, subatomic particles, and what we know today as our universe was formed. Now think back to Wrigley Field with the bases loaded, when that perfect hit cracked through the night became a grand slam and flew right out of the stadium. This resulted in a dazzling display of fireworks and lights at the stadium with the crowds on their feet cheering as loud as they could with all of the excitement of the moment in every single individual. A single baseball became much more than any other baseball that night. It became a legend.

What this does is set the precedence for an object to be the same object in one setting and become something much bigger in another. We wouldn't have seen the same celebration in the stadium if the baseball didn't become a grand slam and win the game. When it was caught outside the stadium, it was instantly more valuable than any other baseball! On the scale of the entire universe, the big bang particle might not have become a big bang unless it became something much bigger. But what made it into the Big Bang from that particle? How did it become so big? Did it get hit "out of the stadium" too? Have we just witnessed a life-changing moment that changes the way we understand the universe? As we will show in this book, the answer to all of these is a resounding yes!

What this suggests is that this "particle of everything" that became the Big Bang may actually have come from another source outside of our universe, like the ball hit from the park. This is a logical course of action because, if our laws of physics are correct, this Big Bang particle could not have existed in the first place due to its instability. In contrast, if the particle came from within a larger stadium and was able to reach past the confines of that stadium just like the baseball clearing the stands, then it could have passed beyond a horizon where it actually became what we know today as the Big Bang – the *creation* of our entire universe! The Grand Slam is the path of this particle before it became the Big Bang. It is the path to ascension for our universe.

What we will describe in this book is that in order for this Big Bang particle to be present in what becomes our universe, with our laws of physics as we understand them, it must have come from a region where it can exist as just a particle, or a region where it is stable. When is a Big Bang particle just a particle? When was our baseball just a baseball? It was inside the confines of the stadium before it became a life-changing moment as it was hit out of the stadium. Inside this stadium, which we will refer to as *the Omniverse*, our Big Bang particle is held in a stable form as just a particle. This particle, the size of a single miniscule point, still contains all of the total energy within our entire universe. When the Big Bang particle leaves its stadium, this is the Grand Slam. The object then enters into a field where our laws of physics now apply, and the creation of the universe begins with a Big Bang!

While so much research about the universe and data collected support the Big Bang Theory, not much has been observed about what happened before the Big Bang because humans focus on what can be seen, measured, and quantified within our universe. The proposal outlined in this book about the *Grand Slam Theory of the Omniverse* does not contradict the process of the Big Bang. Rather, it expands upon the idea.

The purpose of this proposal is to introduce the theory that the Big Bang's source particle was actually stable while it was present in one location. The Big Bang particle traveled outside that location, far enough to escape the enormous amount of energy holding it stable. Once clear of stabilizing energy, it is no longer stable and the Big Bang happens. The objective of this proposal is to: 1) bring awareness to the scientific community of the possibility of an extra-universal object capable on creating and conveying a Big Bang particle; 2) raise questions as to how this process might have occurred; and 3) formulate approaches to test the model presented herein qualitatively.

This work, although enthusiastically titled as the *Grand Slam Theory of the Omniverse*, is not yet a scientific theory, though it is a proposal. According to Steven Hawking, "A theory is a model of the universe or a restricted part of it and a set of rules that relate quantities in the model to observations made." [1] A theory must satisfy the following conditions:

1) It must accurately describe a large class of observations on the basis of a model consisting of only a small number of arbitrary elements; and

2) It must make definite predictions about results of future observations.[1]

It is the ultimate goal of this book to formulate a theory by following these guidelines presented herein. However, it is my purpose to present the proposal. I will communicate the proposal to the scientific community and the rest of the world in order to initiate the following steps of quantification and observation. Hawking also added that the goal of science is to provide a single theory that describes the whole universe.[1] This proposal will describe the universe as a whole with only a few arbitrary elements, and it will make predictions about what types of observations will support it. In the end, I believe this will become a theory to describe the universe as a whole by providing it within a larger framework so one can understand the Omniverse as a bigger picture. This work is not intended to delve into any complex mathematics or formulas. Instead, it is intended to present the subject material in such a way to be easy to understand by any reader. This research will include a detailed description of all known, observed, and measured attributes of the universe from many of history's greatest minds.

Every year, several new discoveries that support the Big Bang and the infinite expansion known to occur in the universe are made, and this study will attempt to find a link. A link as to how the known properties of the universe might relate to the point of origin of the Big Bang. We will refer to the model as the *Omniverse*. 'Omni-', a combined form meaning all, was chosen as the prefix because this proposal looks at the entire process that contains a source of Big Bang particles and enough energy to maintain stability of an unknown number of these particles. Moreover, it contains forces necessary to push this Big Bang particle into conditions where the Big Bang happens.

In other words, the Omniverse is the birthplace of the universe(s) containing all of the collective energies, fields, and matter. Although the Omniverse may be capable of producing multiple universes and parallel universes, this inquiry is not intended to be perceived as a multiverse theory that explains how multiple universes came to be. Instead, we intend to learn about our universe and where it came from, describing the single connection with the source and explaining the process *before* our Big Bang occurred. While other universes may be created in this process completely separate from our universe, it is imperative that the reaction be viewed as a single event throughout the known universe, and everything we can observe in it. Other multiverse theories such as quantum theories are based on solid scientific principles and will be discussed in this book. It is my intention to propose this model within the existing framework of *all* successful theories of the creation of our universe and all that is within.

At this point, most readers might be asking themselves why a geologist would want to attempt to tackle some of the biggest problems of the model we know to be our very own creation. Did you know that the idea of a black hole in space was first postulated by geologist John Michell in 1783, about two hundred years before the first observation? Like many before me, I have a child-like nature and question everything. An education in geology has given me the tools.

As a child in Sunday School, I would be the one who would constantly ask "why" questions. Why did God create the universe? Why did God create planets, and even life? Why were we here? But I also asked where God came from. If God created everything, then it only made sense that there was something even bigger that created God. Who or what created God? I would find out later in life that we are not alone, and we are guided to learn more about ourselves and our surroundings.

After graduating with a degree in geology and starting a career, my curiosity was still insatiable. In my spare time I read books on astronomy, geology, and materials science. My mind was hungry for information and it had to be fed. Even in my dreams I would ponder and ask the universe where it came from. I mentally extended a beam of light from my head with positive energy in hopes that someone or something would come to me and explain how it all happened.

That thought became a life of its own, because something unexplainable *did* happen. Something happened before I had my "ah-ha" moment, and that something that was so simple could be used to explain the process. Then, while watching an astronomy show on TV in the mid-1990s, I saw a presentation of String Theory by Michio Kaku. He proposed that vibrations might be the building blocks for the most elementary subatomic particle, the quark. My interest was sparked. In the closing, Kaku said that "sometime, there might be an equation so simple, that it explains everything in the universe and is only an inch long."

It didn't seem possible at the time, but all of the different fields of study are like pieces of a puzzle that show us how the universe began. When I started putting them together, I realized that a Big Bang reaction *in motion* could occur – and this creates an energy transfer. The momentum from the motion of the universe when the rapid inflation began might have caused these vibrations, like a ball crashing through a window. The ball didn't just appear. This would violate the laws of physics. The ball was hit out of the park!

When it comes to our current understanding of the universe, there is no single theory that explains everything, but there are several theories that explain parts. Think of a picture of our globe with continents spread out all over it. With plate tectonics, we learned that our continents had drifted apart from a point where they were previously a massive supercontinent, as shown in Figure 1. In the same way, the theories of the universe individually look very different from one another, but the pieces start fitting together when you look at the whole picture.

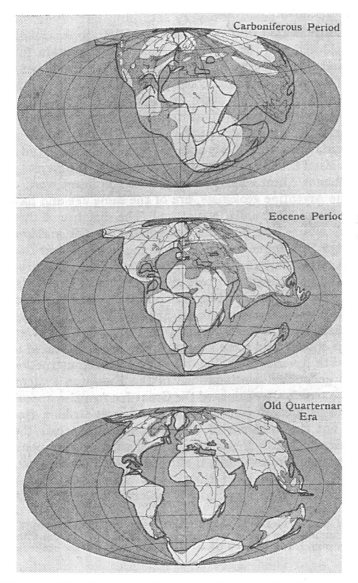

Figure 1, Plate Tectonics: This image shows the breaking up of Pangaea, a supercontinent that existed during the late Paleozoic and early Mesozoic eras, forming about 300 million years ago, and the current locations of the continents today. Copyright: Photos.com, 2013

In the following sections, we will present the laws of physics and theories that govern our universe as we know it, discuss how we make such discoveries, and delve further into the theory of the Omniverse to show how the pieces fit together. What we plan to do with this research is to apply our knowledge of the universe and remove our human constraints such as the concept of time, beginnings, and endings. Instead of a constrained object within space, we shall see that our universe's relation to the larger Omniverse is like a fractal in which a pattern repeats itself. We may ultimately understand the true nature of the meaning of the biblical accounts of how God created us in his own image. What this leaves us with is simply the knowledge that we are just as much a part of the universe as we are of the Omniverse. The connection is always present.

Observation of features in our universe will lead us to observations of our connection with the Omniverse. After learning the concepts of this book, the next steps for the scientific reader will include devising mathematical models to test the theories, and ways to observe and measure energies that may not presently be known to humankind at this time. One important thing to note is that science hasn't yet advanced far enough for humanity to observe all of the energies in the universe. For all readers, this proposal is being presented in order to make a new framework of thought that can be disseminated to specialists of each topic covered in order to formulate approaches to test the model. Also, the concept can be understood by any curious reader. I hope that each person is able to take away a greater sense of being within the universe upon learning these concepts.

Before presenting more details, the background research will be presented in order to show the entire framework of what we know about the universe. Then, each topic will be discussed in relation to the connection to the source object presented in this model known as the *Grand Slam Theory of the Omniverse*. But first, we are going to look into the human psyche of how discoveries are made and what forces of nature help push us in the direction of discovery. A very important understanding of the subject matter of the Omniverse is that we are an integral part of it, so we must first understand ourselves before we look outward. The next section will guide us in this process.

THE ANATOMY
OF A DISCOVERY

"There's a rot of mysterious stuff going on up there."
Dalai Lama the 14th

Why do we discover things? Humanity has always attempted to explain the unknown. Our ancients looked to the skies, observed the patterns, and came up with explanations of how we came to be. Religions addressed the issue, and alchemy went into further detail to explain our role in the universe. Presently, we have modern science that gives us tools to not only observe but to quantify through measurements. In fact, this is the golden age of science in terms of discoveries about our universe and how we came to be.

Why do we have the need to know what happens "out there?" I saw an interview on television with the 14th Dalai Lama who asked this question. Quoted above, he wondered why we must constantly try to understand what is out there in space when there are so many mysteries we could investigate within ourselves. I quoted him to preserve his pronunciation, making light of his accent. So when you read his quote, please hear it in your mind with his voice. It is indeed a very profound question that deserves to be addressed.

The human psyche has a desire and need for discovering how our surroundings work, and doing so gives us a better understanding of ourselves. In other words, we look to the sky and use our knowledge to explain how and why we came to be. You see, every little piece or quantum part of us, including each atom and subatomic particle, was born in this universe and is an integral part of each and every one of us. This is the process of becoming one with our surroundings. And this process is facilitated by discovery. But what does discovery mean to you?

We've all seen it before, and conjured up images of a mad scientist with thick glasses, lab coat, and flowing white hair feverishly working through the night in his laboratory full of beakers and flasks filled with multi-colored bubbling liquids spewing out what looks like some kind of strange fog. He holds up a single test tube to peer through it using the old incandescent light hanging from the ceiling. "Eureka!" he exclaims and he has now officially made the discovery known. While this stereotypical scenario is entertaining, discovery is actually something that can occur in anybody's mind without all of the flashy bells and whistles and scientific mumbo-jumbo. In fact, discoveries are made by everyone every single day.

Me, Myself, and I

We might not recognize everyday discoveries anymore like we used to when we were children. But there's nothing holding us back from doing so but ourselves! How many times have you heard someone saying "find your inner child" and wondered why? Is it because we were innocent? Is it because we loved to play? Or is it because we talked to imaginary friends? The answer is "yes!" Maybe it was because everything we witnessed was like it was being witnessed for the very first time. This sparked a curiosity that made us want to explore, and there is so much more to finding that inner child! Even Jesus knew and taught the importance of being a child in order to enter through the gates of Heaven. If he could go through everything he went through and still be a child, then anyone and everyone can as well, regardless of each person's belief system. Just imagine you are seeing life through a child's eyes and it will happen. Do you remember how big everything seemed and how you constantly changed attention from one discovery to the next? Everything was a brand new discovery!

But as we grow old, we tend to turn off these childlike impulses. We have to deal with "real life," don't we? We sleep, get up, eat, go to work, eat, work some more, come home, eat again, pay bills, maybe work some more, and go back to sleep. This process makes us feel justified in being an adult because we have responsibilities. But then something clicks somewhere in life and we want to be free from the mundane, so we start our own personal journey. Many people have to go through all kinds of seemingly crazy rituals such as self-help seminars, weird diets, meditation, or anything else just to get it back. Just imagine you are seeing life through a child's eyes and it will happen. It is simply the inner child discovering its surroundings naturally.

Another thing we do as we start to grow older is to develop beliefs. Some can be beneficial, but many can harm our personal development if they close our minds to new ideas. It can be stubbornness, or what we perceive as an inability to learn more as we grow old. In fact, we may actually become addicted to our beliefs or disbeliefs. How many of us have ever said "you can't teach an old dog new tricks" before? This is just not true, because that old dog is still a young dog at heart!

For some, beliefs can originate from each person's environment, and others may be from family or community. Beliefs can be passed down from generation to generation or can follow you on a spiritual level, and herein lays the importance of being a child. When you were a child, did you constantly say "that's not real" or "that isn't possible" or try to dismiss anything because you believed in something else? It is not part of a child's thought process to do so! For most children, the discovery *is* truth. We are taught to believe or disbelieve as life progresses. However, it really doesn't matter what belief system we develop in life, or if we decide to dismiss them because discoveries just happen. They happen every day. Are you open to receiving them? You have an update ready to download and install!

"Ok," you might ask yourself, "I can understand the importance of being a child, and even how to do it, but why?" The answer is simple: This child-like form of thought is *pure thought* that another part of you understands. This concept is known as the "higher self" and is analogous to your subconscious. Your higher self is that inner child with the ability to tap into a greater consciousness. Think of it as your "good" consciousness that guides you through successes in life. If you imagine the scenario in which an angel sits on top of one shoulder and a devil on the other, the angel represents the higher self and the devil represents the ego, or the sense of self that gives us self-doubt and facilitates negative thought forms that work against our higher self.

The concept of the ego is not one that needs to be covered in this book, but one can understand this with practices such as yoga and meditation. The ego-driven life dominates our society today but it does not have to dictate how you feel or what you believe. To explain briefly, this is a two-sided pole such as a magnet with its north and south poles. If you are weighed more to one side of the ego or higher self, you can do what is known as a pole shift by aligning yourself with the side of the pole which gives you a greater capacity to live your life. While not everyone seeks this path, the higher self is the part of the pole that typically allows this. I do not advocate abolishing the sense of self, the ego, because it is also an important part of us. Therefore, it is recommended to find a balance on this pole. If you were walking on a high wire holding a pole to balance, you wouldn't hold it by one end would you? As we shall see with the Omniverse proposal, balance is very important.

Depending on what your beliefs are, the concept of the higher self can involve so much more than just what you are physically. When your mind is able to withstand the storm of life and enjoy the quiet calmness that follows, then you experience the higher self. In essence, you are the higher self. You have the ability to think positively and clearly without effort, and are able to act without reacting and stop resisting things that persist. You rise above the mundane parts of your life, and no longer feel the need to please others or yourself constantly. You can just "be." It is living in the present moment, and it is usually described as bliss or nirvana. This state is easily attainable by anyone, not just gurus! Simplify, and let discovery flow through you.

Now that's a lot of concepts for our brains to digest. However, it doesn't have to be complicated. Actually, it's all just a part of what you are. You are you, and you are a child. You are a higher self. They are not separate. It is only our way of understanding that makes us separate things in order to categorize them in such ways. But all of these parts of you work in perfect synchronization, when you let them. And that is a personal journey for each and every one of us in order to find out how that happens. But when it does, life happens!

The Path

So how do we make this happen and how does it affect our lives? Before starting to write this book, I took a class that was taught by an organization that teaches meditation techniques based on what masters have taught themselves for thousands of years. Their purpose was to simplify the techniques so that mediation can be experienced by anyone. I feel as if an enormous weight has been lifted from my mind each time I meditate, and clarity increases. There are too many other mediation techniques available to us today to mention them all. Guided meditations can be found online or at your local bookstore.

After experiencing this for the first time, I started feeling like a child again. Although, I admit, I never really grew up in the first place. I started noticing soon after my first class that the topic of meditation was being reported everywhere in the news and magazines. All of a sudden, everyone was talking about the positive health benefits of meditation. It was as if the universal consciousness was embracing me! If one has a hard time with the concept of meditation, one can merely read about it and focus on the health benefits in hundreds of scientific, peer-reviewed journals in order to understand how beneficial it is. But without arguing any specific quantifiable benefit gained through meditation, I will attest to how I have come to understand my higher self and how I made the most important discovery of my life so many years ago.

As I mentioned before, we work on a higher level to guide ourselves and push us in the right direction. This concept is difficult to fathom for individuals who may hold the belief that God controls our fate. I always took the hard line that I control my own fate. We could all be right. If you are religious, your higher self works with God to push you towards your divine plan. If you are atheist, your higher self might only be a part of your psyche that exists in your subconscious, but the effect of it on your life and well-being is still the same. If you are spiritual, then the possibilities of the higher self are endless and you can witness time break down and the universe just *gives* you the answers. That being said, I now believe that the clarity of mind I am now gaining in life and the path I have chosen to follow is affecting my goals and actions of the past. Now that's just plain crazy, right? Please don't mistake this statement for a scientific principle or anything that I intend to prove, but it is what is known as a "gut feeling." I will show that it is possible.

Think about all of the times in your past when you felt someone was there to help guide you along the right path that led you to where you are today. Now that is heavy. And it gets even better! How many times have we heard that all of our greatest discoveries were by accident? This happens all the time! Some of the greatest scientific advances and technological breakthroughs were just "accidents" that were not an intended outcome. The more you look through our history of science, the more of these "blunders" are found! But if we are to believe that these events were truly by accident, wouldn't we need some kind of proof that the unintended outcome was actually not likely to have happened by replicating the discoveries? For many discoveries, we didn't really discuss how the accident happened, we just accepted it. However, were we ever presented another possible scenario that could lead to the same outcome that wasn't by accident, even though it seemed to the observer that it was?

Let's take a look at the lives of the people that made the great discoveries. Imagine one of your favorite "accidental" discoveries and think about the person or people behind it. They were dedicated and hard working people who never gave up, weren't they? Would you go so far as to say that they were following their own path? The most important concept about discovery is simply following your path. The higher self rewards you, regardless of whether it is some religious concept or just a part of your subconscious. Being in touch with your higher self is how you open the door to discovery.

The Reward

Each of us must experience our own higher self and divine path ourselves. The terms "surrender" or "let go and let God" are popular ways to explain the process. Surrender is the instrument that allows life to play out as you intend it, and with this instrument you can simultaneously play wonderful music, observe yourself doing so, and dance around like a little child. Life is rewarding when you let it be.

I ask myself if I was rewarded with this knowledge in the past, when I had no concept of any of the things I just wrote about. I was so preoccupied with the ego-driven life (based on the sense of self) that I worked crazy hours just to make enough money to pay the bills. It is hard to imagine coming upon an idea that could change our understanding of science in such a little mind. But that's what happened. So do I accept that it happened by accident? I accept that I conceived the idea, but I now realize it did happen for a reason, and that I was guided to a place where the interchange of ideas occurred that were stored in my own subconscious.

The So-Called Unexplainable

I know by now that every reader has to be wondering what the heck I am talking about! What interchange of ideas? How did you reach the "ah-ha" moment? Let's take a look back on the events leading up to my life-changing event that preceded my "ah-ha" moment.

I was unknowingly following my divine path and being guided by my higher self within my subconscious. During college, I left the school of engineering to become a scientist. I found my way to geology because of a fascination with gems and minerals when I was a child. I felt that it was right, even though people tried to talk me out of it. I learned calculus, chemistry, biology, physics, and the history of the universe up to and including Earth's formation. I learned to apply all of the sciences in order to learn our current understanding of life.

Upon graduating and entering the work force, I was still curious all of the time. My curiosity took me to the skies, to understand the nature of our universe. I should also mention that as a child, I was also obsessed with rockets and outer space. As a nerdy adult, I found myself perusing the local libraries for books to further my knowledge. Two subjects in particular that seemed pertinent in some way were the gravitational lensing of light in the universe and quasicrystals, which are crystal-like structures with five-sided symmetry formed in metal alloys. Crystals with five sides usually don't occur in nature and, in order to explain these structures, the mathematical models had to use extra dimensions. This was a huge lesson to me. We do not have to remain constrained to only three dimensions, even if matter as we know it exists in three dimensions.

As I mentioned in the introduction, I would imagine being able to acquire information through higher sources by picturing a beam of light, or a positive streamer, from my head. This would be one of the most interesting parallels to a technique that I learned in 2012, and this was back in the 1990s! Sri Sri Ravi Shankar, through the Art of Living, taught me this technique at a talk I attended in 2012. But it was a technique my mind was practicing back in 1995. Talk about parallels! I believe this led to the eventual subconscious process of communication that came to me in a dream.

But dreams are not real, right? Again, this may be a limiting factor based upon one's own belief system. It is not the purpose of this book to discuss the meaning of dreams, but when a vivid dream stands out in your life as much as this one had, you will remember it and know it was different. I found myself awoken from another ordinary dream one night only to find myself in an unusual place. I could observe my own presence and understood that my physical body was exactly where it lay in bed. But my consciousness was in a unique place with all new sights never seen before in either waking or dreaming states. And someone was there talking to me.

"What do you want?" I asked. "To tell you something," he replied. My consciousness wandered in an attempt to observe his physical characteristics and those of what appeared to be walls surrounding us. I thought to myself, was this thing an alien? Is his face, body, and this room some kind of projection? All of the surfaces in here seemed to be made of rotating polygons that made it look as if it were programmed – even his face. This was before computer graphics in movies had become robust enough to make this possible, so I know it couldn't have been just a dream with fancy graphics after watching too many movies. I thought about the quasicrystals and how they had to be mathematically derived using up to 12 multiple dimensions and thought to myself, is this what it looks like to be able to see more than three dimensions in my mind? It is the eye that translates light from photons bouncing off of three-dimensional objects, and the brain perceives this into what we know as vision. But the mind is also capable of visualizing and seeing that which the eyes don't see. If everything we saw was only through the visual cortex, would we dream or even imagine?

"We are coming," he said with no expression on his face, only the strange phenomena that looked like moving polygons that were projected to make me think that it was ordinary surroundings. I got the feeling that he wanted to give me information in order to help in some sort of transition leading up to a possible contact. It was like a phone call from family saying: "Hi, we're almost there! See you soon!"

Then I went deeper into the experience. This is another parallel to meditation as I understand it today at the present time. I can feel myself sink down a level during a meditation when the conscious slips into the subconscious. I felt pure data as I was surrounded by information. Imagine being surrounded by computer screens, like in *The Matrix* but around you in all directions, where you can see every single screen in your mind without turning around. This was quite different from the normal 180 degree peripheral vision I am accustomed to. It was 360 degrees in all directions. My brain felt like it had a natural connection to this data stream. I wondered, "Is this what the internet will be like?" This preceded my first dial-up internet connection, but the internet becoming part of the public domain was all over the news at the time. I am still waiting for the internet to catch up to this experience!

At the moment my brain felt connected, I was no longer acting from only my subconscious. Like the giant talking flower in *Little Shop of Horrors*, it seemed to exclaim "Feed Me!" I delved deeper into the connection with the intent of finding as much data as I could, as if I were hacking into some supercomputer with my brain. I got through. I was hit with so much information that I "whited out." While still aware of my dream state, I was no longer with anyone nor part of a dream, or even within some other reality. I saw myself floating in pure white space.

It seemed like nothingness, or everything, but it was everywhere. Then time passed by. In such a space, it could have been an eternity that felt like a second, or perhaps a second that felt like an eternity. I was awake in this consciousness and aware of my body and thoughts in the space, and nothing else existed. I remembered that it all started with or within a dream so, logically, all I needed to do was wake up. I am not sure how much time I was in this state, but I did eventually wake up. Wow, what a dream, I thought upon finally waking after a seemingly eternal series of events.

While it is normal for me to remember dreams, or parts of them, I knew this was different and I could not stop thinking that there was some higher meaning to it. But I didn't really have any grand ideas in my head. If information was given to me, it was stored somewhere outside of my conscious memories. The main parts that stuck with me were the projections of the polymorphic surfaces and his face along with the message, "We are coming." I concluded that there was definitely more out there than just human life on a lone planet in a single galaxy inside a universe filled with countless other solar systems. Moreover, it must be possible to initiate some sort of communication on a higher level or higher dimensions without being limited to distances or the speed of light.

Although this situation was completely unique and was not repeated, its concept is no longer foreign to me. I have accepted that we are not alone and if we believe that we are either the only life in the universe or the highest form of life here, those beliefs limit the scope of thought. I didn't need to qualify the experience as alien or anything else because it seemed like doing so would be jumping to a conclusion. I had data and memories of the experience, and that in itself was the purpose. Specifically, the experience showed me possibilities that were higher than what was previously understood by my brain.

Now, with thanks to my present self, I understand that the mind itself is actually a series of fields combined by thought patterns, brain waves, emotions, and even magnetic fields generated from the heart pumping blood with small amounts of iron. So much research today has been done to show that this is in fact the case. Our mind is greater than our brain, and it expands its consciousness outward. That is exactly what I experienced almost 20 years ago!

Angels in the Infield

My present self often reads about and ponders the existence of celestial or energy beings that seem plausible but not quantifiable in a scientific manner, until we have the ability to identify and detect such unknown energies. Currently, we detect forces and energies related to particle interactions that are based on data collected from supercolliders. But is there more to the picture? Angels are a common theme taught to us by the ancients and are mentioned in every religious book since the dawn of civilization. The word "angel" means "messenger of God." I understand them as energies undetected by science, thus far.

The contemporary concept of angels is generally taught to us by psychics or mediums who teach that we are all capable of communicating with the angels. In fact, children often talk to angels and other ghostly entities referred to as spirit guides. If children see them, then is this another belief-based trait we unlearn as we grown older? I often ponder the concept of such celestial beings that on the surface appear to be archaic religious concepts. The odd thing is that they are not really embraced much within a religious framework, except by the prophets.

Angels are everywhere and with every person, trying to communicate with all of us in concert with our higher self. As a scientist, I try to rationalize this phenomenon. Since we typically act subconsciously and think with our conscious brain, I realized that the concept of angels can be explained simply as higher basic thought-patterns within all of our minds. In a way, an angel can be thought of as a higher emotion complete with intelligent thought that is action provoking and goal oriented. These higher intelligent emotions can be triggered with intentional thankfulness, love, and a willingness to do good deeds. Therefore, regardless of whether an angel is an actual celestial being with its own life force or a higher thought pattern within our minds, the outcome of invoking them is the same. Namely, they bring information to those who are open to receiving the information.

In our ancient historical records, Archangel Gabriel came to the Virgin Mary to inform her that she would bear the child of God.

Joseph, who was a widower and took Mary as a second wife, was enraged that she had become pregnant until he was visited by the same angel, who told him that the immaculate conception was indeed true. Archangel Gabriel was also there hundreds of years later to inform Mohammed of his plight to restore Mecca to monotheism. Like other angels and archangels, such beings are not constrained by time or location and exist everywhere at all times – in both sexes. In every one of our lives, we probably had at least one life-defining moment in which we felt we were supposed to do something. Being in touch with an angel means being able to detect higher thought patterns through your self conscious, or subconscious, in order to interpret and subsequently follow a path that is beneficial for humanity and the environment.

It is not from the ego or sense of self, but it is a higher purpose also referred to as the divine path. I often wonder how two scientists can come up with the same theory independently at the same time. This has happened throughout history. It happened with the periodic table. It also happened in many occasions documented in this book's summary on the history of contributions to the fields of physics and astrology. Perhaps they were visited by angels!

The Path, Part 2

Remember how I said you are rewarded by following your divine path? I am now starting to observe what my divine path is as I decipher the messages within my mind to direct me towards goals of service to people and the Earth. I realized that this is why I got into geology years ago and started working in the environmental field. It also has pushed me toward health and safety management in my career, because love for humanity in such a position manifests as safe and happy coworkers.

This divine path has also affected my past. However, my understanding is that the higher self is knowledge gained in my entire conscious and subconscious lifetime. This higher self is not necessarily constrained by time like my body and brain are. In other words, all of the information you receive and all of the love you give in your entire lifetime are your higher self. Moreover, all of that is available to you from your higher self anytime during your entire lifetime.

In conclusion, listen to your higher self, listen to your angels (whether or not you believe, just keep an open mind to higher thought patterns), feel love and gratitude, and follow your divine path. You will find a pole shift within your present time that not only affects the future in positive ways, but also affects the past!

I am confident in believing that not only is this concept possible, but it has led me to what I feel is the greatest single thought of my lifetime: the Omniverse! By applying techniques learned today, such as a positive beam of light from my mind, I observed an interaction with either another being or a higher form of thought within my own subconscious. Through this process, I feel that I was in direct communication with the universe itself, and received so much information that my brain overloaded for an unknown period of time while my body slept through what appeared to be one crazy dream. But the information is real, as you will see.

The Revelation

As I mentioned before, I did not know after I woke if I actually had any information from the exchange. I did not know how much it affected my life either. I just went about my regular day-to-day life of working, eating, sleeping, and partying like crazy on the weekends!

My curiosity for the unknown was still there. In my youth, I always loved a good drunken conversation about what God means to other people versus what it means to me and seeing how we viewed things differently. Sometimes I would find myself in places where I would overhear others having these conversations and just smile and listen in without interjecting my own thoughts.

It was still the mid 1990s. Grunge rock and alternative rock filled the airwaves with thick, distorted guitars reminiscent of 1980s rock but with flannel instead of spandex. I still lived in a party house with two roommates, one of whom was also my former college roommate. We entertained people, cooked giant meals for them utilizing our Italian, French, Cajun, and other recipes in our minds and drank like fish. But through all of this, my mind was always in "ponder-mode." I kept reading in my spare time and watched science documentaries on the television frequently, even though I thought that they were not "cool" at the time. Now I can't get enough of them!

It was on such a documentary when I saw this curious looking Asian man with long, shoulder-length silvery gray hair and a playful voice that obscured the fact that he was some kind of super-genius. He said something that would stick with me to this day. But just as quickly as he made an impression on me simply be watching a show on TV, he was gone. I always wondered who he was, and if I would ever see him again. About 10 years later, I started noticing him on every single show about physics on every single channel out there. Even today, he is one of the top speakers for any show about any kind of science, especially if it involves the future. I see him still with his long gray hair and curious voice as he explains all kinds of scientific phenomena. His name is Michio Kaku, and what he said in the mid 1990s when I saw him is the same thing he says today: "Sometime soon, somebody would come up with an equation so simple, that it would only be about an inch long, and it would describe *everything* about the universe." I was inspired!

Is it possible? Can we really do that? It can't really be that hard if we already know as much about the universe as we currently know! The Big Bang theory tells us how the universe was created, and Einstein's work was simple yet robust. There just has to be something in it that accurately describes the Big Bang and General Relativity together that can be applied on large-scale astronomy and small-scale quantum physics.

Then, suddenly, as if it had just come to me, that moment happened. This was a "eureka" moment brewing within me that there *was* an explanation, but the kicker was that we had not been considering the entire universe in the modern explanations. If there was a larger system that included a source object so large that the universe itself was dwarfed by its presence, then perhaps the entire system is in motion somehow and involves an exchange of energy. This simplified my view of the entire universe that was, and still is, a single point particle – a singularity.

The Vision

My thought started with a vision, not an equation. I could very clearly see a system in my mind wherein pre-Big Bang particles were constantly in motion, building up momentum. I found it to be similar to a solar flare escaping the surface of the sun. Thus, a pre-big bang particle escapes the source object.

I thought about a baseball being hit out of a park and how it would still look like any other baseball, but it would become the almighty Big Bang! I rationalized that if it were moving, we would be able to detect the motion of the universe with all of our sophisticated observatories and satellites. On the other hand, if the universe was a single point particle when force was acted upon it and it developed enough momentum to escape its source then, according to our laws of physics, the forces and momentum of all of the parts after the Big Bang would be equal. I remembered how when I was a child riding inside a car I would toss an object up, expecting it to go straight to the back of the car. I found that its momentum was the same as the car we were in, so it was not affected by forces outside the car.

The idea of the Omniverse was born. It was an all-encompassing creator of infinite universes, which could only be called an Omniverse – the mother of our universe. Like baseballs hit in the air, some particles fall back, some are fly or foul balls, but ours was just right - a grand slam resulting in a perfect Big Bang. The vision in my mind had different fields, similar to inside and outside the baseball field. The Big Bang itself could not work if the pre-Big Bang particle was unstable, but it was. Scientists tell us this. In fact, the Big Bang theory relies on this property to initiate the rapid inflation! So something had to keep the pre-Big Bang particle stable while within a proximity to the source. And just as an object escaping the Earth's atmosphere, the forces (i.e. gravity) acting upon the object are decreased as distance is increased. In the Omniverse, the pressure forces keep the particle stable within close proximity. But as the pressure drops, the Big Bang particle pops!

This model was stuck in my head for many years, only to come out during the occasional conversation about the universe. It has been refined, and analogies I use to describe it have changed over the years. For example, I have found that another analogy is to compare the Big Bang particle to an electron within the electron field surrounding a nucleus of an atom. This is basically a larger version of quanta, like a repeating fractal image. Like an electron, it imparts a charge that balances with the nucleus. The Omniverse may reflect a similar exchange of energy, and help balance the universe.

But my favorite part about this new theory developing in my mind, hopefully to be released someday to the world, was that we were, and still are, in an age of discoveries about the universe. Every time something new was discovered in the last 15 years or so, it often caused the top scientists to have to go back to the drawing board to explain something. But with the Omniverse model already in my head, nothing really surprised me. It all just seemed to fit.

Now that I have the clarity of mind and ability to write and disseminate my thoughts to the rest of the world, it is my hope to apply the concepts discussed in this book to all of the greatest advances and discoveries in the field. Although it is not a mathematical formula, I am starting with a geometric principle of action that looks like a pathway that the universe follows. I am confident that it will encourage our top scientists to apply mathematics to the model in order to formulate hypotheses and determine ways it can be tested and ultimately observed.

Belief

Before we go further, I have presented concepts that may contradict with one's religious or atheist beliefs. Throughout the history of science, many of our greatest minds have experienced similar conflict. Even Einstein was afraid to continue his work because he felt it brought him too close to God, as if we were now doing God's work and understanding what God thinks. More and more books that I read about history's greatest minds show this as a repeating pattern. But I would like to interject that I believe that this process is in our nature, and it should not deter one from seeking knowledge. Snakes slither, spiders spin webs, birds fly, and humans soar. It is natural!

Instead, if there is a God that created the universe and laid the foundation for the beginning of life that evolved to become what we are today, I feel that it/he/she would want to teach us everything and simultaneously learn from us about the knowledge we gain through our perception. In this sense, I do not consider myself to be either religious or atheist. I have found that a balanced position on this pole leads to a greater awareness of my own spirituality, but I do not give others advice or recommendations on what they should or should not believe. However, the tools are widely available for all who seek their own path.

It should be mentioned that my path of spirituality has lifted my awareness of my surroundings and allowed me to constantly ponder such advanced concepts that are presented in this book. Human minds process information in the background all the time, and my spirituality gives me additional tools to interpret the mind. Not only is it my own divine path to experience and explain our origins, but to teach others what I learn and in doing so, advance our understanding as a whole. Welcome to the universal consciousness!

The Hand of God

I would like to send thanks and gratitude for this universal consciousness and explain another vision obtained through meditation. Through an intensive three day course in meditation and silence in January 2012, I found myself lost in a sea of thought. My mind would race and think about all kinds of things but never would quiet down when I needed it to. But unknowingly and even miraculously, this very sea of thought allows me to take in information, as if I were laying in the ocean feeling surrounded by water, absorbing nutrients through my skin. I would get up early, drive more than an hour to Los Angeles where the course was taking place, and then it was in and out of different meditations all day. I honestly didn't know if I was coming or going, awake or asleep most of the time! We underwent guided meditations and learned different breathing techniques throughout each day, practicing silence among each other while still trying other ways to communicate enough to coordinate organized tasks. It was challenging to say the least!

During meditation, it is very typical for the mind to race as it does, and this is natural. I think of my mind as a high-energy dog I saw on the Dog Whisperer, and in order to get the dog to calm down, Cesar Millan took an unexpected approach. He took the dog running and just let it go as much as it could. It worked perfectly, and the dog was then ready to receive instruction. So for those starting meditation practices who try to quiet the mind, just let it go! Once calm, the conscious mind does not realize it has entered a calm state, but it becomes open to receiving information. So we kept going with meditation after meditation for three consecutive days. My knees were sore, my back hurt, I felt my nose hairs growing and rubbing the inside of my nostrils with each breath, and I could smell and feel my own breath on myself. I was becoming aware of myself and the present time without having to think about it. Without having to think about anything at all!

At the end of the third day, the instructor released us from our vow of silence. Having done this before only to be overwhelmed with vocalizations of every student who just couldn't wait to talk again, he was ready for an onslaught of voices and laughter all at once. But nothing happened. We all just looked around the room, each satisfied with our own self, waiting for another to break the code of silence. And we were all happy and content. This went on for a good half-hour, and the instructor gave us all the invitation to say what we wanted all at the same time. It helped break the ice, and when everyone spoke, I also exclaimed the first thing that came to mind: "Thank you, universe."

We shared our personal experiences from three days of meditation and silence among each other. I shared a story of how I saw what I thought was a spirit or ghost on the grounds where we were meditating, which used to be a Christian Science church. He was an aging caretaker who was well dressed as if he were going to the jazz club after work. He wore a nice tweed sport coat, a bow tie, and a derby hat sitting atop his head at a slight angle. I thought about it and I had also heard him play his soprano saxophone on the second day during previous meditations. His beautiful music had penetrated the interior walls of the hall in which we lay, reverberating around throughout the entire building.

I had met this very nice gentleman when I felt myself slipping towards sleep during the third day of meditation, and then I started soaring around the building where my body was. I typically walked laps around the building during breaks to stay active and I was repeating this motion in my mind. I was mentally flying around the building at a faster-than-walking pace and a few feet higher off the ground than my standing height. It was then that I saw this man who smiled a giant, friendly grin and simply pointed back toward the building. The instructor was starting to teach a new technique when I went back to my body, and I would have probably snored my way right through it! I was thankful to have met this gentleman.

But that wasn't all. During the three-day meditation course, I had one very short vision that turned out to be quite profound when I thought about it later. It was simply a hand reaching down to touch the surface of water as one might do in the darkness of an amusement park love boat ride while gently moving forward.

The hand was that of a human, or of the same form. However, the magic happened when the fingers started to move over and touch the surface of the smooth-as-silk water, starting to form ripples.

Just as one would expect by applying scientific principles of motion, the fingers gently penetrated the water's surface and caused beautifully articulate ripples, eddies, and small whirls of currents. That was when I realized that the whirls represented the physical forces in a field of space that form laws of attraction that led to the creation of galaxies, and that this was much more than just a visual from my own imagination. Once again, I was being rewarded with a simple yet efficient glimpse of not only how things in the universe came to be, but also how amazingly simple the method of communication of such a profound idea really is.

The Path, Part 3

And so I find myself at this point in life, writing about my theory and how it happened, but I am still in awe and wonder of how I got here. As I mentioned earlier, I feel that meditation has become an integral part of my life and the path to myself. But what does this mean to the reader? Is meditation a foreign language? Should one try it? Meditation is simply a pathway I chose for myself. Each person's pathway to gain knowledge is their own. Some may find comfort enjoying the numerous health benefits of meditation practice while some might enjoy the relaxation. Some may detest the sitting, lying down, and breathing exercises. Therefore, it might not be right for everyone.

Many may also find comfort with a traditional education system. However, as I have found, we cannot provide all of the answers through traditional systems. Furthermore, as such systems become more dogmatic, it may become harder to question what appear to be very solid theories because some subjects over time generate intense debates. With any system, we always have to deal with people and their belief systems. For those not actively engaged in academics, researching may be hindered by "paywall" sites that charge for accessing research papers. This method may not be right, or economically available, for everyone.

In some cases, we may consider a topic such as evolution a "closed case" and find it difficult to discuss. Most people believe there are two sides to the argument: creation or evolution. When viewed by an open mind, one can realize that they are just two ways of describing the same phenomena that are two ends of the same pole. One way is through religion and another one through science. This creates the illusion of polar opposites with respect to religion and science, but it is only what people choose to believe. Although evolution is based on a scientific principle, it also has many assumptions that one must believe in order to understand the concepts. Such assumptions may one day be overturned with more data. I should stress that there is always more to the picture, but this is really a topic for future exploration since this book focuses on the pre-creation physical model of the universe. This is the Omniverse.

PART

3

THE MAKING OF
THE UNIVERSE

"Whatever you do will be insignificant, but
it is very important that you do it."
–Mahatma Ghandi

Across generations and civilizations, there have always been those
who devoted their lives to studying the universe and the laws of
physics that govern it. While this material could likely be written into
a standalone book or several volumes, a brief summary is presented
herein. We are going to show an overview of the history pertaining
to the study of the universe by summarizing the main points that
have contributed to today's concepts and theories. However, this
is not intended to be a complete history. Rather, the purpose is to
discuss the history's most important points in order to apply it to
the model of the Omniverse.

I have found an excellent summary of detailed contributions
to the field of physics in Steven Hawking's 1988 publication, *A
Brief History of Time*.[1] In addition, during my background research
I found that many other authors have included detailed history
sections corresponding to their work. All of the contributing authors
and publications referenced in this section can be found in the
bibliography at the end of this book.

While my references focus on the modern study of physics, the
true history of the study of the universe and its origins actually precedes
the beginning of written evidence by humankind. Some of the earliest
petroglyphs and hieroglyphs have depicted locations of the stars and
constellations. Modern research has uncovered other advanced finds
such as the Mayan calendar and an early mechanical calendar from the
first century B.C. Even the oldest known civilized society established

some 13,000 years ago and located in modern day Turkey, Göbekli Tepe, has been found to be organized around religion, causing debate over how religion formed in early hunter-gatherer societies.

Göbekli Tepe was built for religious purposes and not around agriculture as previously thought. It is probably no coincidence that studies of this establishment also showed that this is the first known city in the history of civilization. Before science, religion answered questions of our existence and creation. Alchemy then took us deeper into our nature and the nature of the universe. Modern science is currently at a turning point at which we are finally seeing how the universe came to be, but that topic is still widely debated.

For our purposes of historical research, we will start discussing particular categories using examples from great minds that have made significant contributions. The primary theories describe 1) the laws of how the universe changes with time; and 2) the initial state of the universe and include the following:

- Newtonian gravitational and orbital predictions that govern how celestial bodies move in space and time.

- Einstein's General Relativity, also known as *Classical Theory*, which describes the force of gravity and the large-scale structure of the universe. Using Classical Theory, Einstein predicted slightly different motions than did Newton, which were shown to be more accurate.

- Quantum theories that deal with the nature of things on a much smaller scale such as Quantum Mechanics, String Theory, and others. Until recently, quantum theories have not always agreed with classical theory and initially there was no quantum theory of gravity or unified theory of the universe. I will show that quantum theories are not at all difficult to grasp for the casual reader.

- The Holographic Universe, which is part theory of how the brain understands the universe and also presents the universe as a single object with a holographic projection. This projection is responsible for creating everything in the universe as we know it. This involves the principle of entanglement, also known as "spooky-action-at-distance."

The Solar System and Laws of Physics

Some of the first scientific milestones ever made were from the Greek philosopher Aristotle. In 340 B.C., Aristotle wrote *On the Heavens*[2] with the revelation that stars and planets were spherical. This was a major step forward in knowledge, and his theory that all celestial objects revolved around the Earth would persist for nearly two millennia.

In 1514 A.D., Nicholas Copernicus created the solar system model in which the Earth and other planets orbited the Sun. It was widely believed by the church that celestial objects orbited the Earth, so this was viewed as heresy. Catholic rule during this time was very strict and people did not want to be punished for heresy, so it took nearly 100 years for Copernicus' idea to catch on. Then, Johannes Kepler and Galileo Galilei started building public support for Copernicus' theory. Using the newly invented telescope, Galileo observed moons orbiting around Jupiter, which helped support Copernican theory. Kepler modified the Copernican theory in order to show how the orbital paths of planets around the Sun were actually elliptical.[1] Therefore, we had a working solar system model by the early 1600s that included planets orbiting the Sun and moons orbiting planets that has held true to modern times.

The next major breakthrough happened in 1687 with Sir Isaac Newton's *Philosophiae Naturalis Principia Mathematica*.[3] This was much more that just watching an apple fall from a tree, as the legend goes. Newton's work established the modern laws of physics and still retain validity to this day. In fact, Sir Roger Penrose's 2011 book *Cycles of Time*[4] is a detailed proposal for the pre-Big Bang era using the logic of Newton's laws. Newton's laws include the following:

- Newton's 1st law of conservation of energy. A body in motion is affected by force that changes the speed of the body versus force to set it moving. When a body is not acted on by any force such as friction, it keeps on moving.
- Newton's 2nd law of motion. Acceleration due to gravity is always the same, proportional to an object's mass (e.g. twice the weight of an object equals twice the gravity and twice the mass).
- Newton's 3rd law of force. When two bodies interact by exerting force on one another, these forces of action and reaction are equal in magnitude but opposite in direction.

In Penrose's exploration of Newton's laws, Penrose found that laws number one and three are equalities. However, law number two is an inequality. Since the second law equates the rate of change of the motion of a particle, entropy is always greater at later versus previous times in a system. Entropy means that nature tends to go from a state of order to a state of disorder in isolated systems. Penrose added that increasing entropy in the formation of the universe led to the clumping of stars into formations known as galaxy clusters and galaxies.[4]

Thus, Newton established mathematical formulas governing how celestial bodies move in space and time. He also introduced the topic of universal gravitation wherein each body was attracted to every other body, and that the force between the two bodies is stronger when they are closer. Newton was also able to show that gravity causes the Earth's moon to orbit around the Earth elliptically while the Earth orbits similarly around the Sun, thus backing Kepler's previous work.

Finally, Newton demonstrated that without a central point in the universe, stars would not fall inward toward each other into the central point because stars and space are infinite. Conversely, we would observe stars falling into the center of the universe if space is finite. This theory was modified to allow for equilibrium by making gravity a repulsive force at larger distances with an infinite number of stars, which causes regional attraction or repulsion.[1] Today, we have observed several galaxy clusters that form as regional attraction while the universe as a whole experiences expansion.

After Newton's laws were discovered, humanity was looking towards creating a preliminary model of the universe. In 1781, Immanuel Kant published *Critique of Pure Reason*[5], which examined the question of whether the universe had a beginning in time and if it was limited in space. Ergo, was space limited or unlimited? Were there a finite or infinite number of stars in the night sky? In 1823, Heinrich Olbers argued that stars would light up the entire night sky if they were truly infinite unless some mechanism turned them on and off. If stars were infinite, then there would be no gaps between them in the night sky.

Edwin Hubble was credited for discovering that the universe was expanding in 1929. He found that the density of the universe is infinite and it came from a single point. Hubble suggested an infinitesimally small and dense universe in which the known laws of science break down under such conditions. This led to the creation of the "Big Bang Theory."

In 1988 Hawking added that the Big Bang is the beginning of time, and events that existed before the Big Bang can be ignored because they would have no observational consequences.[1] In other words, there would be no effect on the current universe from anything that happened before the Big Bang. Therefore, the universe began at the beginning of time with the Big Bang. I, however, disagree with this assumption and will discuss the reason later. The "Zen" approach would tell us that the past is destiny and the future is free will. I will show that something had to happen initially for the events of the Big Bang to occur.

Classical Theory

Before Hubble's great discovery, a new movement in physics was beginning. The new physics would change the way we view our universe to this day. Discoveries and observations made in the 20th century set the framework for the Big Bang Theory. Even with today's advanced physics, the goal always is to unify with Classical Theory. Let's take a look back at some of the most significant contributions to Classical Theory and see how they helped us determine the concept of the Big Bang Theory.

In 1865, James Clerk Maxwell unified incomplete theories of electricity and magnetism, known as electromagnetism or EM. Maxwell showed that wavelike disturbances in a combined electromagnetic field travelled at fixed speeds like ripples on the surface of a smooth pond. He categorized waveforms depending on their wavelength. The longest known wavelengths are radio waves. As wavelengths decrease, we observe microwaves, infrared radiation, the visible spectrum, ultraviolet rays, x-rays, and ultimately gamma radiation. In addition, Maxwell predicted that radio or light waves traveled at fixed speed. Thus, we now have an official speed limit for light. As far as we know, no matter or energy travels faster than light.

In 1905, Albert Einstein was trying to explain this constant speed of light. He abandoned two earlier concepts. One concept was that of absolute time, a commonplace notion before the Big Bang theory was conceived some years later. The second concept was that of ether in space, an alchemical theory from the Middle Ages. Einstein's *Relativity: The Special and General Theory*[6] (also known as Special Relativity, General Relativity, or Classical Theory) stated simply that the laws of science should be the same for all freely moving observers, regardless of the speed they are traveling in space. This was true for Newton's laws of motion as well as Maxwell's theory of electromagnetic force and the speed of light. Einstein's basis was that the energy an object has when in motion adds to its mass as the object approaches the speed of light.

According to Classical Theory, time is not completely separate and independent from space. Rather, the two are combined into space-time and time is typically used as a fourth dimension along with a traditional three-dimensional system of matter. The fourth dimension of space-time is often illustrated using a blanket-and-ball metaphor. The blanket represents space-time, a two-dimensional, flat plane that is stretched out. A round object such as a ball is then placed on top of the blanket. The resulting effect of the ball on the blanket is that the ball sinks inward, thus curving the space-time "blanket."

After no theory was found to unify gravity and Classical Theory, Einstein in 1914 suggested that gravity is not a force but an effect of space-time not being uniformly flat. He showed that space-time is warped by mass, and that energy follows the closest thing to a straight line in curved space. This causes time to run slower near massive objects. Thus, space-time has the innate ability to expand and balance the attraction of matter.[1]

While Classical Theory predicted that the universe was non-static and constantly changing, Einstein and other physicists were not able to accept this at the time. However, William de Sitter in 1917 used Einstein's cosmological constant to show that the universe is expanding. Widely credited for the Friedmann equations of expansion, Alexander Friedmann in 1922 also predicted that the universe is expanding. Friedman postulated assumptions stating that the universe looks identical in any direction, and this would be true from any point within the universe.

As this expanding trend in physics continued, Georges Lemaître proposed the theory of the expanding universe in 1925. He then followed up with his proposal of the Big Bang Theory in 1927, just two years prior to Hubble's discovery.[1] Hubble is often credited for creating the Big Bang theory. However, other people contributed to the theory of the Big Bang. Hubble documented that expansion was occurring, thus supporting the burgeoning theory.

Hawking in the late 1980s stated that although the universe is roughly the same in all directions, the assumptions made by Friedmann are not necessarily true in reality. However, when looking at large-scale versus small-scale, the Friedmann assumptions were a rough approximation of the universe.[1] Nevertheless, Friedmann's assumptions are used today. With the Big Bang model, many scientists use de Sitter or Friedmann's name when referring to the expansion of the universe that was observed by Hubble in 1929.

The Inflationary Big Bang

Friedmann's models suggest that there was a time during which the distance between all of the known galaxies was zero. Density of the universe was infinite, as well as the curvature of space-time. Classical Theory predicts that there is a point in the universe where Relativity breaks down due to such infinities. This ultimately leads us to the concept of a *singularity* – The Big Bang. It was concluded that the Friedmann Big Bang can occur if Classical Theory is correct.[1]

There were no theories to address what happened before the Big Bang since all we can tell is that it starts from a singularity in which Classical Theory breaks down. Hawking believes that if there were events before the Big Bang, one could not use them to determine what would happen afterward because predictability would also break down at the Big Bang singularity. Therefore, events that may or may not have occurred before the Big Bang would have no consequences and should not form a part of a scientific model of the universe.[1]

We had acquired by the early 20th century Newton's laws of motion, Classical Theory, and the working model of the Big Bang that started from a singularity. The race to match the model with observations then began. As technology increased throughout the 20th century, so did the ways in which we could observe space. Better telescopes, increasingly more accurate technologies, and satellites that were equipped with the latest technology were eventually used to view the universe.

The Big Bang model was developed further over the years throughout the mid to late 20th century. A study in 1948 by George Gamow, Ralph Alpher, and Hans Bethe held that the early universe was infinitely hot and dense with near-zero size. This was known as Planck size, or 10^{-35} meters, the smallest possible size in which any object can be measured.

Temperature is a measure of average particle energy, or speed. Compressing particles increases their temperature whereas releasing pressure decreases temperatures. The 1948 study suggested that photons would have resulted from radiation of this early hot universe, which should still be observable in the universe today at approximately absolute zero (-273°). Gamow suggested that white-hot light from the early universe would have "red-shifted," or transitioned to a longer wavelength, as the universe expanded away from Earth. This red-shifting is similar to the sound of a train moving away from the observer.[1] This light is now observable as cosmic background radiation, or CMB, which was discovered by Arno Penzias and Robert Wilson in 1965 and led to their 1978 Nobel Prize. The discovery by Penzias and Wilson showed that cosmic microwave background was the same in all directions on space. What this means is that the universe is the same in all directions, confirming Friedmann's first assumption.

In 1965 Roger Penrose used Classical Theory with attractive gravity to show that a star could theoretically collapse into a singularity with zero volume and infinite density.[1] This type of singularity, first proposed by geologist John Michell in 1783, became known as a black hole. This type of singularity was also predicted with Einstein's equations by Karl Schwarzschild in 1916. In 1970 Hawking and Penrose wrote that such a singularity had been proven using general relativity. Hawking also added that if one reversed the direction of Penrose's theorem, the collapse became an infinite expansion. Therefore, the Friedmann universe must have started with a singularity. Penrose and Hawking went farther and classified the Big Bang as a partial theory on the basis that Classical Theory was incomplete. They did so because Classical Theory could not predict the beginning due to the fact that all theories break down before time started at the beginning of the Big Bang.[1]

In 1981 Alan Guth also observed that the Big Bang Theory was incomplete. He realized that everything we know about the Big Bang Theory was based upon observation of the events that happened *after* the Big Bang occurred. Thus, in an attempt to explain the "bang," he started publishing on this topic in 1981 and wrote a definitive book in 1997 entitled *The Inflationary Universe*[7] that modified the original Big Bang Theory. Guth built upon principles set forth by Sidney Coleman who proposed in 1977 that the early universe was like a false vacuum that decayed similarly to bubbles of normal space-time, much like bubbles of vapor within a pot of boiling water. Guth proposed that the young universe would go through rapid expansion before returning to the rate of growth proposed by the Big Bang Theory. Thus, the early universe *inflated* at a faster rate than the expansion that occurred afterward. This inflation was nearly instant, occurring in the first trillionth of a second.

Guth also suggested that the temperature dropped below a critical value without symmetries being broken, like super-freezing water without it changing form to ice. This would have made the early universe unstable, and it would possess even more energy than if symmetry would have been broken. This extra energy, like Einstein's cosmological constant, has an anti-gravitational property that effectively creates repulsion. Therefore, expansion accelerates at a rate faster than light can travel.[7] In other words, space unfolded faster than the speed of light at the very first instant of the Big Bang.

The notion of the universe inflating faster than light caused some controversy and more explanations were needed in order to account for the inflation. In fact, one explanation required the inflating universe to break down into bubbles, similar to bubbles in a pot of boiling water. However, this resulted in a non-uniform universe that was different from what had been observed. Andrei Linde and Steven Hawking were able to make the bubbles work by putting the entire universe within a single bubble.[1] This involved all of the smaller bubbles combining to form a larger bubble.

In 1983, Linde was able to use this model without a phase transition during supercooling. Linde used Quantum Theory to describe this with the concept of quantum fluctuations. What he found was that energy in a field that had large spin values due to quantum fluctuations behaves like the cosmological constant and causes repulsion, thus making regions expand in an inflationary way. It was concluded that a quantum theory of gravity was needed to describe the early universe, not the Classical Theory.[1]

Steven Hawking and Leonard Mlodinow's 2010 book entitled *The Grand Design*[8] pointed out real-world evidence for the inflationary Big Bang model. In 1998, mankind experienced a monumental discovery when repulsive forces were observed. Measurements of very distant supernovae revealed that the universe was not only expanding, it was accelerating in all directions from us. Two independent teams of researchers, Riess et al. with the High Red-Shift Supernova Search Team and Perlmutter et al. with the Supernova Cosmology Project Team, had made this important discovery.[9]

Michio Kaku's 2006 book, *Parallel Worlds,*[10] explained new views that have changed the concept of the universe. In support of inflation, Kaku states that the leading theory is the Inflationary Big Bang Theory that Guth proposed in order to modify the Big Bang. However, more questions remain despite acceptance of this model that was verified with observation. What caused the initial inflation? What could have initialized this unknown antigravity force? It is now thought that this same antigravity force is actually causing the continual expansion of the universe that we have observed. In addition, we now know that this expansion is accelerating.[10] As we will see later, the Omniverse proposal will attempt to answer these questions.

But first, in order to answer these questions and understand the contributions that validated the Inflationary Big Bang model, we need to take a step back again into the world of the smallest known objects in the universe. Although the next sections describe many different theories that range from Quantum Mechanics to M-Theory, they can be classified together as Quantum Theory, as I often refer to in this book.

Quantum Mechanics

Quantum mechanics began in the early industrial age when James Clerk Maxwell unified the electromagnetic theories in 1865. The next major breakthrough was Max Planck's *Quantum Hypothesis,*[11] which explained the observed rate of radiation emissions from stars. Now, the need to explain small-scale effects rather than ignoring them led to the development of Quantum Mechanics. Planck dubbed the term "quanta" in 1900 to describe individual packets of light, x-rays, and other waveforms.

Niels Bohr was able to use Quantum Mechanics in 1913 to show that electron orbits were actually a fixed distance from an atom's nucleus. In Bohr's viewpoint, this prevented matter from collapsing in on itself caused by electrons falling back into the nucleus. It was also shown that electrons acted as a wave. An important key property of Quantum Mechanics is that all objects have properties of both particles and waves. Thus, observations in the real world are described in terms using both properties. In addition, Richard Feynman elaborated this approach mathematically in order to calculate orbits in complex atoms.

Note that orbits were calculated, not known. The early drawings of electrons orbiting a nucleus actually misrepresented the atom. The modern view shows that the nucleus is surrounded by an electron field similar to the Earth and its magnetic field. What an atom actually looks like was unknown until 21st century technology allowed for the first photographs to be taken of an atom's nucleus and electron fields.

Werner Heisenberg in 1926 formulated the Uncertainty Principle, which means that scientists don't really know anything for sure! Just joking. Actually, this concept represents a major staple of quantum physics even today. Heisenberg postulated that a quantum of light (a single photon) disturbs a particle in such a way that it cannot be predicted. The more accurately the position of a particle is measured, the less accurate its measure of velocity will be, and vice versa. This is a setback for those who made models of a deterministic, or predictable, universe. But it was a new beginning for Quantum Mechanics as termed in the 1920s by Heisenberg, Erwin Schrödinger, and Paul Dirac, basing it upon the uncertainty principle. Rather than describing particles as having well-defined positions and velocities, they had a quantum state, which was a combination of all possible positions and velocities.

In 1927, Paul Dirac wrote the first paper combining Quantum Mechanics with Classical Theory and by 1928 had formulated the Dirac electron theory.[12] Dirac predicted anti-particles, which are basically an equal but opposite version of any basic subatomic particle. This brings us into the realm of duality in which every particle, wave, and force has its opposite, or what can be thought of as its yin and yang. The positron, or the counterforce of an electron, was then discovered in 1932 and verified Dirac's prediction. Quantum Mechanics became widely accepted during this time. However, it could not be incorporated either with gravity or into the large-scale structure of the universe. Classical Theory was still used to describe the large-scale structure of the universe whereas Quantum Mechanics was used to describe waves and particles on a small scale.[1]

Quantum Electrodynamics

The next milestone came when Richard Feynman was credited in the 1940s with creating the first quantum theory of electromagnetism. This became known as Quantum Electrodynamics, or QED. In QED, the exchange of protons describes attraction between charged particles. Quantum Electrodynamics also explains that fields are made up of bosons that are force-carrying particles that move back and forth between matter particles. Matter particles such as quarks and electrons were referred to as fermions.

An important topic introduced by Feynman was the sum over histories, which means that a particle follows every possible path in space-time.[8] Basically, a particle takes *all* possible paths rather than a single path in order to travel from point A to point B. Thus, the combination of paths we observe represents the most likely scenario.

Electroweak Theory

Scientists continued to look for ways to explain or unify forces together. The next major advancement came in 1967 when two physicists working independently arrived at the same conclusion. Abdus Salam and Steven Weinberg had each concluded that electromagnetism was unified with the weak force. Thus, the concept of the Electroweak Force was conceived. Three new particles known as the W^+, W^-, and Z^0 bosons entered our realm of known subatomic particles.[8]

Quantum Chromodynamics

Due to the limitations of observing particles on the quantum scale, there were not many major observational advances until the advent of supercolliders. Supercolliders are machinery designed to accelerate particles and smash atoms or subatomic particles together so we can measure their byproducts. Yes, we now have subatomic demolition derby! In 1969, Murray Gell-Mann made a breakthrough when he was able to show that collisions with subatomic particles such as protons and electrons produced an even more elementary subatomic particle known as the quark.[1]

Quarks are designated attributes based on different types. First, there are three "colors" assigned to different quarks. These are not actual colors since we are not able to see quarks, just the fingerprints they leave from a subatomic collision. We designated them red, green, and blue in color attribute, and they combine in threes to form a white color attribute. The application of the strong force in quantum physics is referred to as Quantum Chromodynamics, or QCD, which assigns quarks their imaginary colors.[8] In addition, quarks can have six different variations known as "flavors" designated as up, down, top, bottom, strange, and charmed. Flavors have partial charges that, when combined, add or subtract to give a particle its charge.

Protons and neutrons each have three quarks of different flavors but with slight variations. For example, protons are two up and one down, resulting in a +1 charge, whereas neutrons are two down and one up, resulting in no charge. Quantum theory also gives us anti-particles, such as the anti-quark.[1] The contemporary basic concept of particles is that baryons, e.g. protons and neutrons, represent stable particles while their anti-particles and mesons represent force particles.[8] We will explain more about types of particles later in this book.

Group Theory

Another common descriptor of elementary particles is its symmetry, referred to in terms of a particle's spin, or orientation. This concept that became known as Group Theory was introduced in 1971 by John Schwarz, André Neveu, Pierre Ramond.[10] Group theory constrains either massive or massless fields to the spin values of ½, 0, 1, 2, et cetera. A spin of ½ makes matter while spins 0, 1, and 2 give rise to elementary force particles.

Remember that everything in this realm is described as elementary particles and that each force has its particle as well. There are four main categories of forces that are described by their basic force-carrying particles. The weakest known force particles make up gravity. Particles with greater strength than gravity include electromagnetic, weak, and strong nuclear forces. The strong nuclear force is responsible for holding the quarks in a subatomic particle together with gluons.[1]

Quantum Field Theory and Gauge Theories

Group Theory was incorporated with Quantum Mechanics to become Quantum Field Theory, or QFT, in the 1960s after the success of Quantum Electrodynamics. The first breakthrough for Quantum Field Theory was when Feynman renormalized Quantum Electrodynamics. The second breakthrough occurred when Guy 't Hooft renormalized weak interactions. In 1971, Guy 't Hooft was able to come up with a generalization theory of Maxwell's theory of light (circa 1860s) by showing that Gauge Theory was renormalizable.[12]

Quantum Field Theory was followed by Gauge Theories in the 1970s and 1980s, which involved strong and weak energies. Gauge Theories also trace their roots back to the 1860s with Maxwell's theory of light. In 1983, Weinberg and Salaam had made the experimental discovery of the three bosons designated as W^+, W^-, and Z^0 as previously mentioned. In conjunction with Guy 't Hooft's renormalization theory, $W^{\pm}$ bosons were represented as gauge fields in weak interactions.

Grand Unified Theory, or GUT, was proposed as a way to use gauge symmetry that was supposed to unify the electroweak and strong forces. Yet, several features were unresolved. Note that forces are basically varying strengths with different tasks. However, these forces are essentially the same basic underlying energy categorized in order to describe their roles with particles. Still, there have been attempts to unify the forces. The Grand Unified Theory has been widely disregarded in modern physics because the theory does not include an explanation for gravity. However, GUT has given us breakthroughs in physics such as the Higgs Mechanism, which is the act of spontaneous symmetry breaking.[7,13] We will explain the importance of this later.

The Yang-Mills Theory, another Gauge Theory, was successful at unifying known laws of particle physics. However, the theory by itself was not able to explain the current understanding of the universe at that time. Yang-Mills and other conventional Gauge Theories were simply incapable of dealing with gravity.[12] Nevertheless, let's not judge them for their shortcomings.

Renormalization Theory was invented to eliminate divergences with infinite redefinition of certain constants. However, renormalization was in violation of a law from Dirac's success of quantum mechanics that was based on approximation schemes in which each correction term is increasingly smaller. Although most gauge theories seemed to be problematic, 't Hooft was successful in showing how Maxwell's theory of light was generalized to make the Yang-Mills Theory renormalizable in 1971 when he showed that W bosons in weak interactions could be represented by gauge fields. Quantum Field Theory during the 1990s was the most successful physical framework of subatomic particles and forces when Michio

Kaku, a pioneer in the field, published *Quantum Field Theory, a Modern Introduction.*[12]

Quantum Field Theory saw several attempts to renormalize symmetries such as space-time, internal, and Supersymmetry, which made its advent in 1976. Supersymmetry means that properties of a system are unaffected by a transformation such as rotating in space or mirror images, excluding transformation of ordinary space. In this sense, force particles and matter particles are basically viewed as the same thing and each is partnered with the other.[8] As an example, recall how Quantum Chromodynamics explained that quarks were held together with the strong force. Supersymmetry would assign a force particle with each of three quarks in a proton or neutron, as opposed to a Classical Theory viewpoint of forces transmitted by fields. Kaku describes Supersymmetry by referring to it as a symmetry that interchanges all particles found in nature, not just quarks.[10]

Supergravity followed supersymmetry and became the first non-trivial extension of General Relativity in more than 60 years. It was the first theory to combine Classical Theory with a field theory. Supergravity introduced a graviton particle with a superpartner. Supergravity was based on a larger gauge group that made it more likely to have infinities cancel out. This was initially ruled out because the gauge group was not large enough to eliminate all possible supersymmetric counterterms.[12]

The Standard Model

One of the most successful theories from Quantum Field Theory came when physicists set their sights on adding to the Standard Model, or SM, that was established with Quantum Electrodynamics.

Basically, the Standard Model describes all known fundamental particles with the exception of gravity. Even without gravity, the Standard Model is regarded as one of the greatest successes of the gauge revolution.[12]

One of the most important proposals for the Standard Model was from a team of scientists in 1964 that included Peter Higgs, Robert Brout, and François Englert in collaboration with Gerald Guralnik, C.R. Hagen, and Tom Kibble. They proposed the original "scalar boson" and developed the Higgs Mechanism.[13] We will explore and explain the mechanism in more detail in the next chapter.

The Standard Model is a combination of Electroweak and Quantum Chromodynamics Theories that has only recently been able to explain the origins of quark masses or other coupling constants. However, it has been very successful at explaining the particle interactions in particle physics and scattering experiments with supercolliders. Just about every conceivable particle predicted has been observed in supercollider experiments. We will discuss the Standard Model further in this book. The basic point is to introduce the subject of the Standard Model that starts with quarks and the strong interactions of Quantum Chromodynamics.[12]

The Standard Model differs from a more recent quantum theory known as String Theory because the Standard Model is based on actual observed data from supercollider experiments. Such experiments take place at facilities such as Fermilab, CERN, Tevatron, and more recently the Large Hadron Collider, or LHC. String theory attempts to dissect the subatomic particles even further, but is based on theoretical data only, until supercolliders are capable of producing much higher energy than is available today. Nonetheless, String Theory started a new revolution in theoretical physics. And it provides the most robust framework explaining the large and small-scale universe to date.

String Theory

In String Theory, particles are patterns that are similar to vibrations of a string of infinite length. It is a beautifully simple concept that entices us romantically to listen to its wonderful music while learning about the universe. Yoichiro Nambu, Tetsuo Gotu, Leonard Susskind, and Holger Nielson had each identified the key feature of a vibrating string.[10] Just as playing a violin string can make several notes, string theory tells us that different vibrations make up different types of subatomic particles and forces. Thus, an underlying energy or vibration makes up quarks and all other particles and forces.

String Theory introduces the concept of multiple dimensions that go beyond our typical view of three space and one time dimension. It describes ten dimensions, some of which are infinitely curved in on themselves, thus making the extra dimensions too small to observe. The concept of duality in String Theory was introduced and showed us that different string theories and different ways of curling up extra dimensions basically describe the same phenomena in four-dimensional space-time.[8]

Michio Kaku and Keiji Kakkawa performed early work contributing to String Theory in 1974. Kaku and Kakkawa extracted a field theory of strings that summarized the entire string theory into a simple equation in two dimensions. As described by Kaku, a one-dimensional string can be viewed as a simple line, or a two-dimensional string can be pictured as a straw. The first dimension is the length of the straw whereas the second dimension is curved around the straw.[10]

In 2005, Leonard Susskind and James Lindesay quite literally wrote the book on String Theory. Susskind and Lindesay took a simpler approach in the definition of strings in their publication entitled *An Introduction to Black Holes, Information, and the String*

Theory Revolution, The Holographic Universe.[14] In this description, a string is a one-dimensional as opposed to a four-dimensional continuum whose points are continuous parameters. Susskind and Lindesay also wrote that String Theory provides a microscopic framework for statistical mechanics.

Susskind set out to solve Hawking's 1976 dilemma of black holes involving information loss, which has since been conceded by Hawking.[8] In order to address this paradox, String Theory competed with Quantum Field Theory to compare to a string near an event horizon of a black hole using light cone quantum mechanics.[14]

The event horizon marks the point at which nothing can escape the gravitational force of the black hole. Susskind found that the information stored in a system falling into a black hole would be spread out all over the event horizon. Thus, information is not lost. An observer outside the black hole would actually see an object as a string diffusing over an increasing area of the event horizon as time progresses. The object falling into the event horizon on the other hand would seem fixed and finite when observed from its viewpoint.[14]

A string would look like a plane propeller to an outside observer who sees it diffusing. Moreover, other propellers would appear at each end of the propeller blades with additional propellers on the ends of those, and this process repeats itself as the object is spread across the event horizon. If an observer were brave enough to accompany an object falling into a black hole, he or she would not see what the other observer sees. In essence, time would slow to a near halt for the observer falling into the event horizon. Thus, the information is not lost in this scenario.[14]

String Theory was followed by Superstring Theory. However, this required one "commonsense" notion of the universe to be let go and replaced with an alternative theory. Those notions included continuity, causality, unitarity, locality, and point particles (i.e.

electrons). Locality means that there is no guarantee that Quantum Mechanics would hold true when the universe was only a Plank-sized particle before the Big Bang. However, there are no successful alternatives to Quantum Mechanics to date.[15] That is, until the Omniverse is studied further.

Superstring Theory abandons only the concept that elementary constituents of matter are point particles. The theory does not change the current understanding of continuity, causality, unitarity, and locality. In 1984, Michael Green and John Schwartz were able to show that Superstring Theory was anomaly-free by using the most robust possible model of unifying gravity, known as E_8. The simplest way to describe Superstring Theory is that it unites forces and particles in the same way that a violin string provides a musical description of musical tones. Ergo, one string can explain all of the notes that you hear when it is vibrating in different frequencies.[15]

Green and Schwartz were able to show that Superstring had no inconsistencies, mathematical divergences, or anomalies. Thus, they were making this theory the best-known "theory of everything" during that time. The most realistic of the String Theories known to us today, called Heteroic String, actually incorporates Grand Unified Theory and the Standard Model.[10]

However, String Theories had their problems because they were based on theoretical science that is not observable in the real world. To complicate matters, there were as many as five string theories describing the same phenomena. Without a complete theory combing Quantum Mechanics and gravity, humanity has set its sights on achieving this task. Hawking wrote that a new Quantum Theory should follow these requirements:

- A new Quantum Theory should incorporate Feynman's sum over histories in that a particle follows every possible path in space-time. Histories should be added up not only in real time but also in imaginary time with a negative value such as "backwards" time that is indistinguishable from directions in space. This results in an effective cancellation of space-time, or a universe without time[1].

- Einstein's curved space-time caused by gravity that is based on Euclidean four-dimensional geometry, but space-time should also incorporate imaginary time.

- In order to make predictions, we must calculate the possibilities of different states of the entire universe at the present time.[8]

A new school of theories would emerge in the mid-1990s and revolutionize String Theories. This was a brand new movement in science. This is M-Theory.

M-Theory

Although there were many different versions of String Theories, they eventually became part of M-Theory, which can be referred to as Membrane Theory or the mother of all theories. M-Theory built upon Superstring Theory as well as the Supergravity concept from Quantum Field/Gauge Theories. Thus, this new set of theories would provide a bridge between the theoretical string theories and classical relativity. M-Theory was the first group of theories to combine large-scale and small scale formulas describing the universe as a whole.

Although M-Theory theory is based on the most recently constructed models of the universe, M-Theory can trace its root back much further because it actually began from an accidental discovery made in 1968 regarding work that had been done back in the 1800s.

As the story goes, Italian theoretical physicist Gabriele Veneziano and Japanese-American physicist Masatsugu Sei Suzuki found that Leonard Euler's Beta function from the 1800s satisfied the mathematical requirements to describe observed particle scattering.[15]

There was no way Euler could have known how significant his Beta Function was since particle scattering was not a technology readily available until the 1960s. Euler also did not know what contribution it would make to the field of science. Therefore, work on your vision regardless of whether you know how much of a contribution it will make. Even if something is less significant in the present, it may become more important in the future. Hence, the quote from Gandhi at the beginning of this chapter: "Whatever you do will be insignificant, but it is very important that you do it." Euler did not know what contribution he was making at the time, but that did not stop him. Contemplate whether the discovery by Veneziano and Suzuki might not have been by accident. Perhaps they were meant to discover it.

M-Theory made its way into physics in the 1990s by using Superstrings to unify Quantum Field Theory and General Relativity (Classical Theory) using Gauge symmetry. Its official inception was in 1995 when Edward Witten and Paul Townsend discovered that five different ten-dimensional string theories were all different ways of "slicing" an eleven-dimensional object.[10,15] This was a major breakthrough in physics.

Now we can describe a string as a one-dimensional "slice" of a two-dimensional membrane that vibrates in eleven-dimensional space-time. A membrane as introduced in M-Theory is commonly compared to a drum head that vibrates in different tones, similar to a string that vibrates in order to play all of the notes. I like to think of it as the roll of the kettle drums in an orchestra. As we can surmise, the universe is made of music. One might go so far as to describe the observer as a great conductor of beautiful music who interacts in concert with the universe. Next time you step outside, listen closely and interact. You can hear divine music everywhere!

One of the individual theories incorporated into M-Theory is that of Supersymmetry. This theory asserts that particles are not actual particles but instead are ten-dimensional vibrations that have length but no height or width.[8] Maxwell's 1994 concept of duality was used to describe how many different string theories were really just different ways of describing the same four-dimensional structure. Supergravity as a concept of supersymmetry is related to the other string theories in this way. Thus, M-Theory incorporated five different string theories including Supersymmetry and Supergravity into a single, unified theory with the addition of an eleventh dimension[15].

M-Theory used more allegories than that of vibrating strings to describe physics. The theory also used one-dimensional point particles, planes of two-dimensional membranes, three-dimensional blobs, and other objects up to nine dimensions that are known as p-branes.[8,15] P-branes can be referred to simply as a brane, or with the number of space dimensions. For example, our universe with three space and one space-time dimension would be called a 3-brane.

Steven Hawking and Leonard Mlodinow's 2010 publication of *The Grand Design*[8] marked a milestone in the direction of quantum physics by effectively endorsing M-Theory. M-Theory is defined by Hawking and Mlodinow as "a family of theories, each of which describes observations within a subset of physical situations (with some overlap)."[8] Michio Kaku also made significant contributions to M-Theory and provides information about its history and concepts in *Introduction to Superstrings and M-Theory*.[15] He writes that the fundamental physical and geometric principles and actions of M-Theory are unknown. Thus, it is considered a top-down theory as compared to the usual bottom-up approach.

A bottom-up approach 1) describes the theory from beginning to end, as does the standard model of physical interaction; and 2) uses laws of physics in order to calculate how history develops with time.[8] For example, we usually start a quantum theory by writing down the geometry or symmetry of the theory and then writing down the action. This action is then used to make predictions about the theory.[15] Conversely, in the top-down approach, the following conditions apply:

1) The laws of nature are apparent, depending on the history of the universe
2) For different histories, the apparent laws are different
3) The number of large dimensions (e.g. four-dimensional space-time) is not fixed by any set of the laws of physics
4) For every large space-time dimension, there is a probability of amplitude assigned to it, ranging from 0-10; and
5) Parallel universes exist with *all* possible internal spaces.[8]

Yes, String Theories and M-Theory have brought us into the day and age wherein parallel universes are accepted within the scientific community.[10] As Hawking and Mlodinow wrote, we accept the notion that the universe exists with all possible internal spaces with a top-down approach and that the relative probability amplitudes for similar universes are testable.[8] Therefore, M-Theory brings the realm of parallel universes into the light of possible reality. Additionally, multiple universes can arise naturally from known physical laws. This basically applies Feynman's sum over histories approach to the universe as a whole. Therefore, each universe has many possible histories as well as many potential future states.

The mathematics of M-Theory allow for different universes with different apparent laws and as many different internal spaces as 10 to the power of 500. That's a 1 followed by 500 zeros. In this sense, there may only be a few states of universes such as ours. Thus, it is assumed that most universes would be unsuitable for life.[8] But looking at the big picture, we can hypothesize ways in which to predict and make observations if parallel universes are testable. This could be just what String Theories need to be validated.

To summarize, M-Theory has successfully incorporated the following theories:

1) Quantum Mechanics
2) General Theory of Relativity
3) Grand Unified Theory (GUT); and
4) Supergravity.[15]

Universes with eleven dimensions are typically viewed as having three large "x, y, and z" dimensions, seven curled dimensions, and one time dimension. The curled dimensions are generally regarded as being unobservable due to their curvature. The precise shapes of these dimensions are determined mathematically by the value of physical quantities and by the nature of the interactions between elementary particles. It should be noted that stable orbits are possible within three large dimensions by following Newton's laws of motion. However, the orbits would be unstable with more than three. In addition, gravitational attraction between bodies decreases with increasing numbers of dimensions.[8] This may ultimately help explain why gravity is so much weaker when compared to electromagnetic, weak, and strong forces as physicists attempt to solve the Hierarchy Problem.

M-Theory currently represents the best possible explanation for all of the known laws of the universe. However, its actions are unknown because it is a top-down theory.[15] Therefore, it is an incomplete theory without simple geometry and leaves the theory in an obscure state. In addition, it has the same weakness of other String Theories in that it has yet to have any observable features. However, we are now in the day and age where supporting observations are being made, and discoveries are not too far away.

Supporting Observations for Quantum Theories

Quantum Theory made major leaps forward in 1992, 2001, and again in 2013 when the Cosmic Background Explorer (COBE), Wilkinson Microwave Anisotropy Probe (WMAP), and the European Space Agency's Planck satellites respectively captured images of the very early universe, each with even greater detail and accuracy. All three images from the different satellites showed that the temperature, now red-shifted to cosmic microwave background, was very uniform because it was in a state of thermal equilibrium, but it had slight variations of the intensity of the radiation with different directions. These slight variations in temperature, as shown on Figure 2, were quantum fluctuations. Thus, quantum fluctuations of the early Big Bang have now been observed.

At this point, we can see the success of quantum physics today. It has been successful in predicting near uniform temperatures with slight fluctuations, and this is exactly what was observed in all three attempts. The tiny temperature fluctuations correspond to regions of slightly different densities at very early times of the Big Bang. This represents the seeds of all future structures including stars and galaxies we observe today.

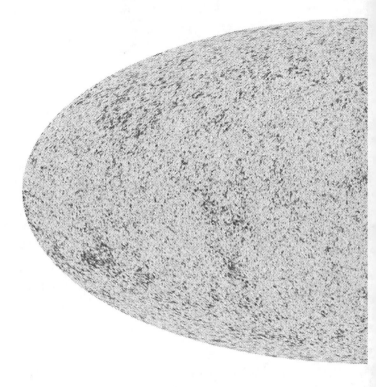

Figure 2 Cosmic Microwave Background: The European Space
map ever created of the cosmic microwave background, the
of features that challenge the foundations of our current
months of data from Planck, this is the mission's first all-sky
sky when it was just 380,000 years old. This young universe
electrons and photons at about 2,700 ºC. When protons
set free. As the universe has expanded, this light today has
a temperature of just 2.7 degrees above absolute zero. This
fluctuations that correspond to regions of slightly different
future structure: the stars and galaxies of today (Copyright:

Agency's Planck space telescope acquired the most detailed
relic radiation from the Big Bang, revealing the existence
understanding of the Universe. Based on the initial 15.5
picture of the oldest light in our universe imprinted on the
was filled with a hot and dense soup of interacting protons,
and electrons joined to form hydrogen atoms, the light was
been stretched out to microwave wavelengths equivalent to
cosmic microwave background shows tiny temperature
densities at very early times, representing the seeds of all
ESA–Planck Collaboration, 2013).

In addition to these findings, we now have a more accurate age of the universe that was refined in March 2013. The European Space Agency's announcement of the Planck telescope's findings showed that the estimate was 13.82 billion years, which is just slightly older than the previous estimate of 13.75 years from the WMAP findings. By analyzing the data, we have determined that the universe contains only 4.9 percent ordinary matter, followed by 26.8% dark matter, and a whopping 68.3% dark energy. Dark matter can be observed by indirect effects of gravity, and dark energy is the force proposed to explain the accelerating expansion observed in our universe.

Dark Energy and Dark Matter: The 95% Universe

Dark Matter is known as pressureless, non-relativistic matter that interacts weakly with matter particles of the Standard Model. Dark Matter was initially conceptualized when the Swiss astronomer, Fritz Zwicky compared dispersion velocities of galaxies with the known observable masses of the stars in the galaxy in 1933. What he found was that more mass was required in the galaxy in order to support the observed velocities. Today we know that Dark Matter does not mediate the electromagnetic force, and Dark Matter can only be inferred from gravitational forces. In other words, Dark Matter does not give off either light or heat. Dark Matter typically clusters by gravitational instability, but it does play a very crucial role in the growth of galaxies and galaxy clusters.[9]

A 2006 observation of Dark Matter from the Bullet Cluster was photographed from the Chandra X-Ray Observatory. The Bullet Cluster is actually two clusters attracting each other and passing through one another. A cluster is a large group of galaxies, so this is much bigger than just a few galaxies colliding. The Dark Matter was not in the picture but was observed by using red-shifting techniques in order to color normal matter red and Dark Matter blue in a photograph taken by the Chandra X-Ray Observatory. The matter, which typically consists mostly of gases, interacts when the galaxies slow down toward the center of the colliding cluster. The dark matter does not interact and simply passes right through, which leads to a wider path than that observed of ordinary matter. It should be noted that some matter such as stars and planets would be able to pass through without colliding with anything. However, the weight of galaxies is actually mostly from the gases, which are affected more than dark matter.

While we have proven that Dark Matter exists and has measurable effects, it has yet to be explained. Explanations for possible Dark Matter candidates are currently debated, and several experiments are being conducted to attempt to explain what constitutes Dark Matter. Some theories suggest that if the universe is a flat projection, dark matter could be on a parallel projection. This parallel world doesn't interact with photons in our realm, but gravity linked to the underlying forces of nature exists throughout all dimensions. Thus, it could be extradimensional matter that we don't see. String theorists have predicted superpartners in Supersymmetry. Although few superconductor experiments have been able to detect superpartners to date, it is theorized that these particles would have mass and may account for Dark Matter. We have observed neutrinos changing flavors, but only three times. Thus, more evidence is needed.

Other experiments aim to detect Weakly Interacting Massive Particles, or WIMPs, either indirectly or directly. At CERN, the first round of results from the Alpha Magnetic Spectrometer, or AMS, were announced in April 2013. According to the press release, antimatter in the form of positrons has been detected and measured. The positrons may originate from Dark Matter in space. If you are an aspiring scientist, Dark Matter is a great field to study. There is a Pulitzer Prize just waiting for someone to come along with an explanation.

Dark Energy was discovered in 1998 by the two teams of Riess et al. and Perlmutter et al. Their independent research demonstrated that the universe is not only expanding, but also that the expansion is actually accelerating. This heralded a new era of physics in an attempt to explain this new phenomenon. According to Luca Amendola and Shinji Tsujikawa's 2010 textbook entitled *Dark Energy Theory and Observations,*[9] Dark Energy is distinguished from ordinary matter species such as baryons and radiation because it has negative pressure. Such pressure leads to accelerated expansion by counteracting gravitational force.

After its discovery, Dark Energy was estimated to comprise more than 70% of the energy in the universe. The remaining components include Dark Matter at about 25% and "normal matter" at approximately 4%.[9] Estimates have been refined using data from the Plank Space Telescope in 2013 to about 68%, 27%, and 5%. All of the progress to date in classical relativity and quantum theories basically gives us an understanding of 5% of the universe. We're still working on the other 95%.

There are several candidates in the race to find an answer to the newest problem in physics. Namely, what is Dark Energy? Einstein's 1917 cosmological constant concept is the current contender, if not the reigning champion. Ironically, Einstein had devised this mathematical formula in order to realize a static universe within the framework of Classical Theory. Einstein later recanted the cosmological constant, claiming it to be one of his biggest blunders. Almost 100 years later, this concept is still being used to describe how Dark Energy might work.

The cosmological constant is basically vacuum energy density. What this means is that there is an energy value that permeates the empty vacuum of the universe. This value can fluctuate, resulting in regions of attraction or repulsion. However, the cosmological constant is typically a large value and therefore problematic in mathematical simulations.[9]

During the late 20th century, the cosmological constant was resurrected first by physicists working on Inflation and later String Theory. Within the framework of String Theory, it is possible to construct a De Sitter vacuum using a tiny cosmological constant. To do this, extra dimensions are compacted with very many available fluxes (10 to the power of 500) and non-perturbative corrections.[9] Note that the amount of available fluxes is as many possible parallel universes that were predicted in M-Theory.

There are two basic approaches to Dark Energy models, both of which simply modify the top or bottom of one of Einstein's equations:

1) To modify energy-momentum, known as modified matter; and

2) To modify gravity, also known as modified gravity.[9]

In 2000, Gia Dvali, Gregory Gabadadze, and Massimo Porrati used the second approach. In their calculations, the late-time acceleration of the universe can be realized as a result of gravitational leakage from a three-dimensional surface (known as a 3-brane in M-Theory) into a fifth extra dimension.[9] Surprisingly, this approach is also used to explain other phenomena that will be described in the following section.

Higher Dimensions and the Hierarchy Problem

There are parts of contemporary physics and history that generally remain unknown, unless one delves deeper into the subject. While many involve concepts of Quantum Theories, many of the theories discussed below can trace their roots back to Classical Relativity and its progenitor, Albert Einstein. One such page in history begins with a letter written to Albert Einstein by Theodor Kaluza in April 1919. Remember that Einstein added the fourth dimension of space-time to our traditional three-dimensional structure of matter. What Kaluza found was that if this approach was taken a step further, Einstein's equations could be applied in five dimensions. When Kaluza applied Einstein's equations in five dimensions, he found that Maxwell's theory of light was consistent in the fifth dimension. Moreover, this was observable via ripples in the fifth dimension that correspond to light waves in four-dimensional space-time.[10]

It was later found that by applying the same principles in even higher dimensions, $W^\pm$ and Z^0 bosons and gluons could be calculated from the weak and strong fields. This led to the concept that such higher dimensions were possible. Additionally, the higher dimensions can be curled up and actually compacted into a space smaller than an atom.[10] This concept was used to describe additional dimensions in String Theories, and today M-Theory incorporates these innovations of thought.

In my background research, I also found many "new-age" titles using the concept of the fifth dimension. This opens up a world of possibilities for a theoretical thinker. Moreover, the concept of higher dimensions also has more applications that are used today in order to explain real physical phenomena such as gravity. Gravity has been one of the biggest problems to explain using traditional Classical Relativity and Quantum Mechanics approaches.

Lisa Randall, a professor of Theoretical Physics at Harvard, has used a higher-dimensional approach to explain the nature of gravity. Strong, weak, and electromagnetic forces at the beginning of time are all roughly the same order of magnitude in the Big Bang.[10] So where does that leave gravity? Although it is theorized that all four are variations of the same underlying energy, gravity is actually much weaker than the other known forces of nature. For example, a small magnet can pick up an object, out-competing the gravitational force of the entire planet. This is generally referred to as the Hierarchy Problem in physics, which starts with gravity but includes much more in particle physics. Lisa Randall has an explanation for the Hierarchy Problem.

In an eleven-dimensional system consisting of five large dimensions and six small curved dimensions, the fifth dimension actually attenuates gravity. Thus, gravity is stronger in the higher dimension. However, in our dimensions gravity appears weaker than the strong, weak, and electromagnetic forces.[10] This is known as the Randall-Sundrum Model after Lisa Randall and Raman Sundrum collaborated to theorize a fifth-dimensional explanation of the weakness of gravity in 1999.

Randall and Sundrum were trying to solve why the other three forces are so much stronger than gravity. The two came to the solution of a five-dimensional universe that contains a four-dimensional brane by applying the concepts of M-Theory. A brane is similar to a membrane, but with more dimensions. If a membrane is two dimensions, the brane can be visualized as a blob in four dimensions. This is how our universe is described in Einstein's Special and General Relativity, but in this approach it is referred to as three space dimensions and one time dimension.

Lisa Randall's 2006 book entitled *Warped Passages*[16] describes the theory. Two branes are used. One is the gravity brane in which gravitons exist. The other is the weak brane in which all the other elementary particles reside, otherwise known as our universe. The weak brane is three dimensions of space and one of time. It is where Classical Theory exists. The two branes are separated in the higher dimension and carry opposite energies. This gives us the effect of a warped fifth dimension.[16] Further work on this model modified it to show that the fifth dimension is infinite rather than a fixed length.

So how does this help us answer the hierarchy problem of gravity's weakness? Using superstrings that attach to the branes, gravity is just as strong as the other forces in the higher-dimensional gravity brane. But as gravity crosses over to our four-dimensional brane, it is attenuated and weakens. Randall and Sundrum used this separation to propose that the strength of gravity is as strong as the other forces, but only until it reaches the weak brane.

How did they explain this? Basically, all the fundamental particles and forces are represented as open strings with the exception of gravity and its particle, the graviton. Strings that are open must be attached to a brane, or they must be closed strings as the graviton is represented. The open strings have their ends stuck in our brane. Therefore, they cannot extend into the fifth, warped dimension. Thus, all we see is in our universe is three dimensions of space and one of time. Forces and particles are strings with open loops leaving them attached to our brane, and gravitons are represented as closed loops that exist both in our brane and in another brane. The other brane is the warped fifth dimension.

Using the Randall-Sundrum Model as a guide for predictions, it may be possible to detect strings in experiments in the near future by using the Large Hadron Collider if there is enough energy to run such experiments. In early 2013, the Large Hadron Collider underwent modifications to increase the energy available for such experiments. We may find experimental evidence for String Theories and M-Theory utilizing this approach.

It is my belief that further studies in String Theories and other dimensions will lead us to advances in understanding Dark Matter. I had often pondered whether it could be higher-dimensional matter that interacts with gravity but does not interact with light. With Kaluza's calculations, light appears in our four dimensions and leaves only ripples in the fifth dimension. Furthermore, in the Randall-Sundrum theory, gravity appears weaker in our four dimensions and stronger in the fifth dimension.

In addition to such ground-breaking physics, there are other well-studied yet not so well-known topics that have nonetheless contributed to current known theories of the universe. In one example, Einstein made an effort to disprove Quantum Mechanics because he viewed it as a competing theory to relativity. However, he strengthened quantum theories because his experiment provided data that now supports the theory that the universe may actually act like a holographic projection which is able to transmit information faster than light.

Spooky-Action-at-Distance

Let's take another look back into Einstein's work and how obscure discoveries were made that changed the way we currently view our universe. I found a great description of what may be Einstein's most bizarre experiment in Kaku's *Physics of the Impossible*[17] and wondered why this was not common knowledge in every book. This is the story of "spooky-action-at-distance," also known as quantum entanglement.

After the success of General Relativity in Einstein's career, he held strong to his ideas. So strong, in fact, that he wanted to disprove Quantum Mechanics because he saw it as competition for his work. Late in his career, Einstein considered Kaluza's fifth-dimensional concept as a way to strike back at Quantum Mechanics. After that, he had attempted to squash the competition. However, this attempt may have backfired.

Einstein in 1935 teamed up with Boris Podolsky and Nathan Rosen in what was later named the EPR experiment, which stood for Einstein, Podolsky, and Rosen collectively. I think that there should be a movie about this. The three scientists' proposed experiment had the purpose of killing off the introduction of probability in physics. Einstein was quoted as saying, "The more success the quantum theory has, the sillier it looks." [17] Silly, perhaps, but quantum physics is still here today, and stronger than ever.

The EPR experiment started with two electrons that were initially vibrating in unison, also known as being in a state of coherence. What they found was that the two electrons could remain in a perfect wave-like synchronization, even with large distances separating the electrons. It was found that even at light-year distances, some kind of invisible wave still connected both electrons allowing them to communicate seemingly faster than light. This was referred to as an invisible Schrödinger wave, so named after one of quantum theory's earliest contributors to the uncertainty principle.

If something happened to one electron, information was immediately transferred to the other one. This phenomenon became known as "spooky-action-at-distance" or Quantum Entanglement.[17.] Quantum Entanglement is a subject of interest for many new age books and articles today. For many people, the concept of entanglement is a very important principle in describing humanity and the state of the universe. We will come back to this issue after we further discuss the experimental data.

To understand entanglement, let us take a look at the properties of the electrons. The total spin of a system with two electrons is equal to zero, or with one electron "up" and one "down." However, according to the principles of quantum theory, electrons exist in all possible spins before a measurement is made. Therefore, each is simultaneously up and down. Once a measurement is made, this wave function collapses and leaves the particles in a definite state.[17] This process is similar to taking a snapshot of the two electrons.

The actual information exchange at the time they are measured is faster than the speed of light. Because the wave functions of the two electrons are in unison, they were thought to be connected by an invisible "thread." Einstein coined this as "spooky-action-at-distance." In his mind, this would prove quantum theory wrong because nothing can go faster than light.[17] The underlying mechanism that they were trying to disprove is the concept of probability.

Further studies were conducted on the Einstein, Podolsky, and Rosen experiments but were not very commonplace. In 1972, John Bell attempted to show that two quantum particles in contact with each other initially would show that separate measurements would not be equal. Bell's "inequality" as it was known was based on his notion that one measurement would be larger than the other would. In his theoretical experiment, the particles were entangled if two separated particles were to violate his principle of inequality.[18]

The 1980s may bring back memories of New Wave music, strange styles with weirdly-thin ties and parachute pants, and movies like *Back to the Future* in which a mad scientist builds a time machine from a Delorean sports car. This sounds like a recipe for some fun! Alan Aspect and his colleagues during the 1980s actually were working to replicate the Einstein, Podolsky, and Rosen experiment. Aspect's team produced results that agreed precisely with quantum theory after they measured photons emitted from calcium atoms. I never thought I would say this, but Einstein: Fail! It should be noted that although Aspect's team did show that information was transmitted at speeds faster than light, the information was essentially random.[17] The most important finding from this experiment was that Aspect had shown that the photons were entangled, thus replicating the results of the EPR experiment.[18] "Get in the car! There's no time to explain!" came to mind while I researched this subject.

Another key experiment using Einstein, Podolsky, and Rosen's spooky-action-at-distance had come out of the 1990s. New Wave was dead and Grunge Rock ruled the airwaves. Styles changed from parachute pants to baggy flannel clothing. Nevertheless, some people still preferred lab coats. A research team at IBM led by Charles Bennet was working on teleporting atoms using the techniques from the EPR experiment. They did this by teleporting the information contained in each particle. This was followed by teleporting information contained in photons, and later, cesium atoms.[17] In the news and all over the young internet, photographs were distributed that were taken by electron microscopes showing an IBM logo made with individual atoms. By 2012, researchers were photographing individual atoms and molecules as technology progressed.

Today, Quantum Entanglement is still being experimented with. A team of Chinese researchers has duplicated tests demonstrating entanglement of particles and gone further than previous studies. In 2012, they broke the quantum teleportation distance record. Then, the Chinese team in 2013 measured the speed of entanglement at four orders of magnitude faster than light. Although the modern equipment used cannot measure exactly, the research team was able to say it was over 3 trillion meters per second, or about 10,000 times the speed of light. In addition, researchers were proposing experiments in April 2013 to test entanglement aboard the International Space Station. Their purpose is to develop the first quantum communication network.

Quantum Entanglement is even being used to solve dilemmas of black holes. Scientists announced that the so-called firewall paradox of the black hole's event horizon was solved in 2012. In a black hole there is an inner and outer event horizon, and quantum teleportation is used to describe what happens as information is exchanged when objects pass through the outer event horizon. Remember that information can never be lost. The field of Quantum Information Theory has now emerged. Quantum Information Theory is a modern branch of quantum mechanics that treats light and atoms as carriers of information. This is another great field of study for aspiring scientists – a field that will one day bring quantum computing into reality. Can you imagine a faster-than-light internet?

Virtual Particles and the Holographic Universe

Another concept Hawking and Randall have each written about is that of virtual particles.[8,16] These elementary particles, paired with their antiparticles, move in and out of existence as each forms then they annihilate each other in a continuous loop. This process indirectly changes the energy of electron orbits.[8] Basically, something can exist as both a particle and as an anti-particle. Its existence is a cycle that is romantically involved in an eternal self-repeating pattern, like a Yin and a Yang. The quantum concept of the sum over histories tells us that this is indeed such a case, when allowing for all possible variations of a particle's existence. This would be a good basis for the notion that each basic fundamental particle consists of a "pixel," and that this particle can turn on or off while existing in all states. Next, visualize that the universe is full of pixels and picture the universe as a hologram. A hologram is a projection with the entire image contained in each individual pixel.

A very little-known revolution using the principle of Quantum Entanglement was occurring in the early 1990s. A year before his early death at age 38, Michael Talbot completed what would be his life's work entitled *The Holographic Universe*.[18] This would build upon the EPR experiments by comparing the universe to a holographic projection. It also delves into the human psyche of perception and understanding because the human brain also functions like a hologram. In Lynne McTaggart's foreword to the 2011 edition, she describes a hologram as a quantum filing cabinet in which the information, or files the cabinet contains, is being stored or folded into quantum waves.[18] This is similar to the invisible waves or threads that allow particles to remain in an entangled state via instant communication.

Talbot describes everything that we perceive as projections from a level of reality so far beyond our own that it is literally beyond space and time.[18] While his work may seem to be ahead of his time, Talbot documented the works of scientists that had actually been working on this in the early 20th century. Quantum physicist David Bohm and neurophysiologist and author Karl Pribram had been the primary researchers in Talbot's work. Bohm and Pribram independently arrived at their own conclusions in which the universe and the brain each operated under conditions that were similar to a holographic state. It was also found that the Holographic Model explains many other mysteries such as telepathy, precognition, psychokinesis, and the mystical feeling of "oneness" with the universe.[18]

Note that many of these important discoveries occurred with independent people or teams performing research. Perhaps there is more to this principle of quantum entanglement than Einstein had thought! For anyone interested in further studies of the universe, our perception, and our ability to understand these topics, the concept of a Holographic Universe is a great endeavor that many conventional scientists have not dared to explore.

Next, we will look at what the pixels of the universe can become. We will discuss the fundamental particles used to build bigger particles. This concept is the framework of all observable data within today's world of quantum physics. This is the Standard Model. Well, the name may not have much pizzazz. Nonetheless, it is an important topic. I just think that maybe it could have been called the Uber Model, or something even better. After all, the Standard Model in physics is akin in importance to the Periodic Table in chemistry. The Standard Model consists of the fundamental building blocks of all of the atoms in the Periodic Table and the forces that affect them.

When we discuss how the models work with the concept of the Grand Slam Theory of the Omniverse, we will compare these areas of study to see how they fit within this proposal of the Omniverse model. I will close this chapter simply by saying: To know the universe is to know one's self.

THE STANDARD
MODEL
DECODED

"Unification and simplicity have been the eternal
Holy Grail of physicists and artists."
—*Alan Lightman*

The Standard Model of physics is basically a description of particles. Since everything has particle properties, this makes for a simple approach. In addition, since we use particle colliders to discover and observe new and existing matter and force-carrying particles, the Standard Model has withstood the test of time with countless observational data. The way physicists visualize and describe subatomic particles is typically by the effects each particle leaves behind from its collision.

The basic building blocks of matter are called molecules. These are repeating patterns of varying atoms held together by different types of bonds. They key concept to remember is that the atoms and bonds in molecules make repeating patterns, like a crystal lattice for example. The components of all atoms are subatomic particles called protons, neutrons, and electrons. As the field of quantum theory progressed, even more fundamental building blocks than just subatomic particles were found. Each subatomic particle is a combination of forces composed of smaller, more elementary particles.

Protons and neutrons are referred to as baryons and are made of three quarks each. On the other hand, electrons consist of a single lepton. These are the tiniest known building blocks of subatomic particles. There are different generations of quarks and leptons, but they are generally grouped into what is called fermions. The fundamental forces of nature include gravity, weak and strong nuclear forces, and electromagnetism. Each has its own force-carrying particle, such as the graviton, gluon, boson, and photon. This is the less than 5% universe we can observe.

Although the Standard Model is not complete and still has problems to be worked out, the Standard Model is currently the most successful theory, or group of theories, that describe quantum particles. Its success is due to the fact that particles can be predicted and observed. The Standard Model has been shown to be successful because its predicted particles can be tested by using supercolliders such as the Tevatron, Fermilab, or the Large Hadron Collider, or LHC.

Supercolliders accelerate and smash particles together, thereby measuring the energy signatures of the byproducts resulting from collisions. When this happens, we use detectors to capture data from the byproducts and use them to generate a graphic representation. Each generation of supercollider is built with better technology to provide higher energies for experiments. The latest generation supercollider, the Large Hadron Collider, is being reworked until 2015. It will provide the highest energy to date in hopes that more of the Standard Model will be verified.

The Standard Model describes almost every known piece of matter and force-carrying particle. With the exception of gravity, or the graviton, and supersymmetric "s" partners, most have been observed. Supersymmetry predicts that every particle will have a superpartner, but the energies required to observe these are higher than technically feasible. That is, until the Large Hadron Collider comes back online.

A good example of a recent success story from collision experiments at the Large Hadron Collider is the Higgs boson. An example of an event producing a Higgs boson is shown on Figure 3. The discovery of the Higgs boson was announced on July 4, 2012, and verification of the findings was announced in March 2013 after several months of analyzing the data. This was one of the missing puzzle pieces for the Standard Model because it verifies the Higgs Mechanism whereby particles acquire mass.[13]

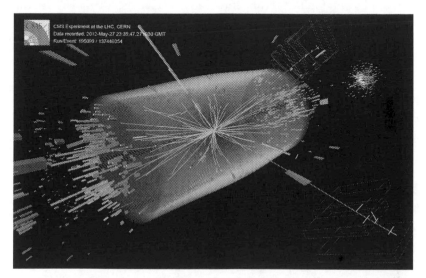

Figure 3 The Higgs Boson: Event recorded with the CMS detector in 2012 at a proton-proton centre-of-mass energy of 8 teraelectronvolts (TeV). The event shows characteristics expected from the decay of the SM Higgs boson to a pair of Z bosons, one of which subsequently decays to a pair of electrons (line upper left and towers on left) and the other Z decays to a pair of muons (lines upper and lower right). The event could also be due to known standard model background processes. Copyright: CERN, 2013

The field of particle physics is always growing. New materials are being developed and tested that allow the superconductors, which typically operate near absolute zero, to be operated more efficiently at slightly warmer temperatures, although still quite cold for humans. Larger supercolliders with higher energies are planned for construction as older ones are placed out of service. The latest generation supercollider, Large Hadron Collider, has already yielded incredible results, as shown by the discovery of the Higgs boson. The Large Hadron Collider will continue to amaze us during its lifetime of operation, considering that what we have seen from it so far is just the beginning.

One could go on about the methods used to produce results, but it is already well studied and documented. A good knowledge of statistics is needed to understand the methodologies, and it gets really fun when rigorous statistical methods are applied to verify the data. But rather than going into these methods, I tend to look for the results. In addition, descriptions of the particles and interactions categorized by the Standard Model can fill up huge volumes themselves. This section is not a complete view of the Standard Model, but what I have done is touch on the important concepts that pertain to the Big Bang model, which will be discussed in the next Chapter. Now we will look at the fundamental particles that are relevant to our work, and we will see how they stack together.

The Standard Model's Contributors

Force-carrying particles include bosons ($W^\pm$, Z^0, and Higgs), gluons, photons, and gravitons. These particles move back and forth between matter particles while transmitting forces. The four basic forces are electromagnetic (EM), weak, strong, and gravity. In the electromagnetic force, photon exchange occurs when a fermion (i.e. electron or quark) recoils after emitting a boson. The boson then collides with another fermion that absorbs the force, thus changing the motion of the particle.[8] The introduction of three bosons known as W⁺, W⁻, and Z^0 bosons came with Quantum Electrodynamics (QED). Quantum Chromodynamics (QCD) introduced gluons as the force-carrying particles that are literally glue holding quarks together with the strong force. The key concept to remember is that fermions consist of quarks and leptons whereas the force-carrying particles are photons, bosons, gluons, or gravitons.

The Standard Model's particles and redundancies can also be described in terms of string theories. In Supersymmetry, for example, the distinction of fermions and bosons is determined by the particle's spin value. Bosons, gluons, photons, and gravitons have spin values of 1 or 2. Fermions, on the other hand, make up the building blocks of matter and have a smaller spin attribute of ½. Fermions are paired with the boson force-carrying particles. This concept is known as having a superpartner.[10] Just like a superhero's sidekick, it is always there.

However, superpartners are too massive to be produced in supercolliders because of the limitations of energy involved in supercollider experiments to date. Perhaps they want to keep their identities hidden in a manner similar to superheroes! An important piece of evidence for Supersymmetry does exist, though. Electromagnetic, weak, and strong forces in the early Big Bang are all roughly the same order of magnitude at the beginning of time.[10]

In Quantum Chromodynamics, quarks are bound together by the strong force via gluons. Quarks and anti-quarks are given attributes such as "colors" with "red, green, and blue" varieties. These "colors" must combine to form white. Additionally, they have six flavors of "up, down, top, bottom, strange, and charmed."[8] Let's take a look at Figure 4 to imagine what quarks might look like with three colors and six flavors.

The Standard Model Matrix

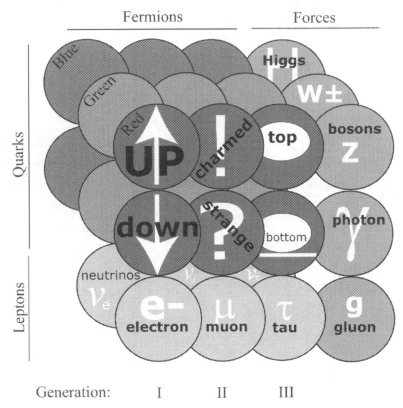

Generation: I II III

Figure 4 The Standard Model Matrix: A unique look at the Standard Model with the different types of colors and flavors of quarks.

As shown, there are eighteen different varieties that combine in various ways to form subatomic particles! When quarks are paired with an anti-quark of different colors, they make mesons. Three quarks or anti-quarks combine to form baryons that, depending on the "flavor" of the quarks, can make protons and neutrons. Do you remember when you were told that nothing else existed and protons and neutrons were the most fundamental particles in an atom's nucleus? Quarks of different attributes including colors, flavors, and spins combine in different ways to form these particles.

One might ask the question, how do quarks attract each other and how do they form a particle instead of just colliding? The answer is a term called asymptotic freedom. This means that strong forces between quarks are greater when the quarks are farther apart than when they are closer together.[8] Therefore, by settling into the form of a subatomic particle such as a proton or neutron, the three quarks have settled into a state with less energy than if the quarks were floating apart from each other in space. Thus, the proton or neutron is the preferred state of three quarks, since it takes less energy to be in that state.

The Higgs Boson Discovery

Where were you on July 4, 2012? Who knew that on this day scientists would reveal the announcement of a new discovery that would change the landscape of science as we know it? It caught me by surprise not only because July 4th is a holiday in America, but it also landed in the middle of the week. I would have probably made the announcement on Friday because you know the scientists were all going to party after the announcement! But they all went back to work on Thursday, hangover or not. I, on the other hand, was getting ready to start a fire on the grill to slow smoke some barbeque with mesquite charcoal and watch some fireworks. Meat, veggies, marinade, fire, beer, great monumental discovery, and fireworks – we've got them all! Wait, a great monumental discovery? What is this? Higgs Boson discovered? Cue the fireworks and Tchaikovsky's 1812 Overture!

What was this announcement and why was it so important? This was what physicists had been talking about for decades, and unbeknownst to me, it was the holy grail of sorts, describing how particles acquire their mass. This one particle was so important that almost the entire Standard Model relied on its existence. It could literally make or break the model. Predictions of the Higgs Boson – the so-called God particle – were already emerging in publications and books. Hopefully, it will be taught in science textbooks in the not-too-distant future. The announcement was (drum roll please): The Higgs Boson has been discovered with overwhelming evidence that it exists, meaning the experiments were replicated enough to achieve statistical accuracy. While the particle itself was not observed, the team at the Large Hadron Collider demonstrated that it clearly exists because of the signature, or fingerprint, it left in its decay pathways. It was clearly the particle scientists had been looking for, and it is a monumental success for physics and the Standard Model.[13]

When the announcement was made that there was now enough data collected to meet rigorous standards for particle physics experiments, scientists came to Lisa Randall for a description of the Higgs Boson, Higgs Field, and Higgs Mechanism. In her book, *The Higgs Discovery,*[13] Randall describes how these three concepts are interrelated. The reason this discovery became so important is that it is a huge success for the Standard Model, validating some of the most fundamental theories that the model is based on. The Higgs Mechanism gives particles their mass. According to Randall, a particle's mass can tell us two things:

1) How a particle responds to forces, and
2) How a particle travels through space.

Thus, we can now "read" some of the underlying particle's properties such as resistance to an applied force. It is mass that gives us this resistance.[13]

Although this particle has also been referred to as the "God Particle," this may have only been termed that way by the media in order to bring it more attention. It was actually named an explicit version of that by physicists trying to observe the elusive particle! Its real identity is named after physicist Peter Higgs. I often wondered if they called it the God Particle because it is responsible for particles having mass – so maybe it makes particles go to church so they can have mass. Bad joke aside, this sounds like the perfect place to sing the music of the universe! Now we understand one of the most basic properties of matter. Rejoice!

As Randall describes, there are three concepts involved in this discovery. They are the Higgs Boson, Higgs Field, and Higgs Mechanism. The Higgs Mechanism is the process that can give elementary particles their masses. The Higgs Boson is a particle that the experiment is designed to seek out. However, it should be noted that it is very difficult to find them in these experiments. Nevertheless, the Higgs Boson has definite mass and interactions. The Higgs Field is a concept that came from Quantum Field Theory (QFT). The Higgs Field is a non-zero quantity that permeates the "vacuum" of space. This gives all of space a non-zero value, like an electromagnetic charge but different. Thus, the field – or charge – is responsible for providing the root of elementary particle masses.

The Higgs Field is responsible for giving particles their masses, not the Higgs Boson.[13] The field exists throughout all space, making the concept of "empty space" obsolete. Space is always filled with energies! The Higgs Field provides a quantity that exists throughout space and permeates the vacuum of ostensibly empty space with a value that is not zero, in a similar fashion as the mysterious Dark Energy, which will be discussed later in this book. Therefore, empty space isn't really empty at all. What we describe as a vacuum is space within this non-zero value field. This is similar to an electromagnetic field.

You might not feel a magnetic field or a Higgs field, but they are present nonetheless. We just don't know yet if the Higgs field carries measurable energy such as electromagnetic charges. In the case of the Higgs field, it doesn't carry an electromagnetic charge, but it does carry another kind of value. It allows particles in this field to have mass. Thus, energy carried by empty space has measurable consequences such as gravity in Einstein's theories or Dark Energy. Dark Energy causes the accelerated expansion of the universe.[13]

Why is it so important to know what causes particles to have mass? As we shall see in the next chapter on the Big Bang, an important time in the universe's creation involved particles attracting each other. Mass is the key to the power of the attraction between all fundamental particles. It is also fundamental in the Hierarchy Problem in physics. Before full atoms were constructed, basic atoms that were made of just the nuclei, such as deuterium (or heavy water), were forming. Having a mass, in addition to a charge, leads to the ability of the nucleus to bind with an electron and create complete atoms. Mass balances the attraction and forces prevent the atom from collapsing inward on itself. Therefore, particle attraction is fundamental to our knowledge of how matter came to be.

How does it work? It starts with fundamental particles that are able to experience the weak force. These particles include the Higgs Boson and also weak bosons, quarks, or leptons (i.e. electrons). The particles interact with the Higgs Field and acquire a "charge." This is not an actual electromagnetic charge but similar to a charge from the electromagnetic field, hence the quotes. This charge from the Higgs Field only has a short range. Such is one of the properties of the weak force.

When we look into the process a little further, we see that each individual particle's reaction with the Higgs Field determines how much mass the particle will have. Particles actually have a wide range of reactions with the Higgs Field, resulting in the level of interaction with the field. In addition to *The Higgs Discovery*,[13] Randall discussed the theoretical Higgs Mechanism and the Hierarchy Problem in an earlier book entitled *Warped Passages*.[16] Her work is essential to understanding the Standard Model.

When a lepton or Higgs Boson particle interacts with the Higgs Field, it acquires a charge. Such particles acquire a non-zero mass when they interact with the field. A key concept to remember is that its mass is determined by the level of interaction with the field. The Higgs Field experiences the weak force. In addition, there may be two Higgs fields. The Higgs Field(s) evenly distribute the weak charge throughout the universe. The particles known as weak gauge bosons interact with the weak charge in the vacuum of space. Thus, the charge that exists everywhere in the vacuum has a dual functionality. Not only does it give particles their mass, but it can also block the particles from communicating these forces over long distances.[16]

Since low-energy particles can only communicate forces at short distances, heavier particles are identified with shorter range distances of weak force. What this does is make it look like weak force symmetry is preserved at short distances but broken at larger distances.[16] This suggests that a particle becomes heavier if it communicates less with the field.

Why was this infamous little Higgs Boson particle so important to find if the field is what gives the particles their masses? The discovery of the particle validates the theories of the Standard Model and proves that this is indeed the mechanism by which subatomic particles gain their mass. The Higgs Boson particle gives us a signature or fingerprint that tells us that the Higgs Mechanism does exist in our universe. Therefore, the field must be present everywhere.[13] Additionally, we are one step closer to discovering the underlying mechanism for gravity. A particle has been predicted in Supergravity, but we still have yet to observe the elusive graviton.

An important concept involved in the Higgs Mechanism is that of broken symmetry. This sounds like it could be the title of a movie! In this analogy, a pencil is often used to describe broken symmetry. Think of a pencil standing on end and look directly at its end. You will see that the pencil is the same when rotated. This is because it is symmetric. Since the pencil has six sides, it can be rotated six ways and still look the same. In addition, when the pencil is standing, its potential energy is higher because it is going to fall. When it falls, it can go in any direction. Therefore, we are no longer able to rotate the pencil on end. Thus, symmetry is broken. Broken symmetry means that the symmetry is no longer exact.[16]

Note that because the pencil is lying on its side, its symmetry is broken. In addition, the pencil in a fallen position is in a lower energy state. The non-zero value or "charge" of the Higgs Field is actually a lower energy state. Thus, it makes the preferred pathway for the interaction.[13,16] To sum this up, a Higgs field of zero is similar to a standing pencil that can fall in any direction, thus breaking symmetry and leaving a "charge" in the field. Compare this to a north-south arrow that indicates a magnetic field. The pencil falling actually seems like a three-dimensional arrow similar to the one-dimensional arrow of a magnetic field. It points to a direction, like a compass, indicating that the field is in a non-zero state.

Note that the Higgs Boson particle hasn't been detected, but its fingerprint has. Why haven't we detected the particle? It quickly decays and consequently creates other particles as decay products. The two primarily observed modes of decay include the following daughter products: 1) photons, and 2) weak gauge bosons. More theoretical decay pathways exist, but these two decay pathways are what the experiments have targeted. Of the two categories, only the gauge bosons are susceptible to the weak force. However, the mechanism applies to electromagnetic force with regards to photons. Since the photons do not experience the weak force, they cannot gain any mass. A third, less frequent decay pathway of the Higgs Boson results in a bottom quark. This also carries electromagnetic and strong force charges. However, it can become neutral with a bottom anti-quark. In other words, it is very difficult to observe this type of decay. It just blends in with all of the background noise from the detectors.[13]

There is one more trick that the Higgs Boson has up its sleeve in order for this mechanism to work, thus resulting in particle masses. A particle created by the field must have a spin 0 value because the vacuum does not preserve symmetry. This means that the charge of the field does not change with regard to direction. This makes sense since the Higgs Field is the same in all directions. Therefore, assuming that the Higgs Field actually does carry a charge the value cannot be conserved because the charge disappears into the vacuum due to its symmetry.[13] Picture the pencil analogy just one more time. Once the pencil falls, it no longer has the potential energy that it had when it was standing on end. Thus, the pencil has less energy, or the value is not conserved, when it breaks symmetry and falls into its current non-zero state. But when it was standing, the potential charge existed everywhere, because the pencil can fall in any given direction.

The Higgs Boson's discovery, verifying the existence of the Higgs Mechanism and the Higgs Field, allows us to address one of the most basic attributes of a subatomic particle, its mass. The next step in logical order would be to produce an observation of gravity using the graviton as the force-carrying particle. Mass and gravity go together ever since the earliest laws of physics were being tested. Laws, for example, state that force equals mass times acceleration. Note that a weak mass scale determines the particles masses because the mechanism involves the weak force. This weak scale is much smaller than the Planck scale that is typically used in order to determine the strength of gravitational attraction. Testing for particles on the Planck scale requires energy levels much greater than what we can produce in supercollider experiments today. Turn the collider up and let's go! The hunt is on.

PART 5

THE BIG BANG

"Take the past as destiny, future as free-will and be happy in the present. A foolish person looks at the past as free-will with regret, future as destiny and is miserable in the present."
—*Sri Sri Ravi Shankar*

We may not always agree on theories of how to explain large-scale versus small-scale phenomena. We have seen a divide in quantum theories and Classical Theory as well as gaps regarding our understanding. Yet, we have a remarkably simple and elegant view of how the universe began that now combines both approaches. M-Theory now incorporates modern String Theories and Classical Theory and has been used to modify the original Big Bang Theory with the concept of inflation. Inflation is the "Bang of the Big Bang" because it occurred instantaneously when the Big Bang started.

The Beginning of the Universe

In the beginning, 13.82 billion years ago (±1%), the universe was infinitely dense and hot. Since all of the energy of the universe was in the form of heat, there was no rest-energy. Thus, the early universe was essentially massless.[4] It was only a Planck distance across (10^{-35} m), which according to Hawking is "the scale at which quantum theory does not have to be taken into account."[8] This is the smallest known amount that can be measured. The known laws of science break down under such conditions, resulting in the Big Bang. At 10^{-12} (0.000000000001) seconds, the temperature is in excess of 10^{16} (10,000,000,000,000,000) degrees. As Penrose states, "relevant physics becomes blind."[4] This is literally the first instant of the Big Bang. This energy spurred the instantaneous inflation of space, and the Big Bang followed.

An important note about the theory is that space-time starts upon inception of the Big Bang. Although the Big Bang is typically thought of as an explosion, it was not. The Big Bang is now described as a rapid inflation because the universe is observed to be uniform when compared to what would have occurred with an explosion. Inflation is a rapid expansion or projection of space-time. It is like turning on the television and seeing all of the pixels light up at the same time. All high definition channels all the time, and it's free! Let's tune in.

Inflation

Alan Guth explained the concept of rapid inflation at the time of the "bang" that is known as "time zero" in the Big Bang Theory, based on quantum theories and M-Theory.[7] The rapid expansion caused by inflation was not completely uniform. This unconformity produced miniscule variations of the temperature of the early Big Bang, what we now observe as cosmic microwave background (CMB). As we discussed in Chapter 3, our picture of the early universe's temperature by COBE, WMAP, and the Planck Space Telescope showed that the nascent universe was indeed uniform, though with slight variations in temperature. Inflation provided adequate time for the temperature in the early universe to equilibrate.

So what is this inflation that is otherwise known as rapid expansion? Kaku describes it by stating that the universe initially expanded faster than light via antigravity force.[10] Since it is assumed that space-time can't move faster than light, Guth's model states that the rapidly inflating universe was actually empty space with "bubbles" of space-time that resembled bubbles in boiling water.[7] These bubbles combined and our universe became a large bubble with four dimensions of space and one of time. This resulted in our universe that is now part of this veritable boiling pot of water within a bubble that appears "flat" when compared to the universe as a whole.[10] Therefore, the universe as a whole was built upon additional dimensions. However, we may have a set amount of dimensions in our bubble.

Another way of describing our bubble is with a brane, a concept from M-Theory. Think of a two-dimensional membrane or a three-dimensional blob. A brane can be any number of dimensions and carry a charge.[16] Our brane is three dimensions of space and one of time. The areas surrounding our brane are not limited to the same number of dimensions as our universe. The universe is inside our bubble.

There was no matter formation during the rapid inflation of the early universe. There were four dimensions of space and none of time at the beginning. This is the reasoning we use in order to describe that time zero started at the Big Bang. The early universe was thus uniform, almost smooth, had slight variations or irregularities, and had four dimensions of space.[8] The rapid inflation of the early universe must have appeared to be a great flash if one were able to observe it. Similar to a sonic boom, the faster-than-light expansion known as inflation would have resulted in a flash of light once photons formed and were able to move freely throughout the cloud of primordial particles. Let's take a look at how this rapid expansion or inflation unfolds itself.

The Radiation Epoch

Within one second of the Big Bang, the temperature falls to 10 billion degrees. Small particles start to form. The universe now contains photons, electrons, neutrinos, and their antiparticles. A neutrino is a lepton, like an electron, with a spin of ½ but no charge. It is generally referred to as a weakly interacting subatomic particle. However, matter as we know it had not yet formed at this point because only a few protons and neutrons have come into existence. The temperature decreases by half each time the universe doubles in size. Therefore, it is also dropping in temperature as the universe is expanding. Electrons and anti-electrons annihilate each other and leave photons behind. This provides a near balance of elementary particles. Neutrinos and anti-neutrinos are able to survive without canceling each other because they are only susceptible to gravity and weak nuclear forces.[1]

The one-second milestone of the early universe marks the beginning of what Guth calls big bang nucleosynthesis.[7] This is also known as the radiation-dominated epoch.[9] The energy density at that point was five million times that of the mass density. The energy of electromagnetic radiation had not spread evenly throughout space, but it was concentrated in photons. Inflation occurred quickly and resulted in near-thermal equilibrium as the universe became supercooled, resulting in a gravitational field. The supercooled universe resulted in a false vacuum that was unstable, thus allowing the exponential expansion. As the vacuum decays, inflation comes to an end and gives way to a slower rate of expansion. This decay of the false vacuum is compared to bubbles in boiling water in which each bubble represents a normal vacuum.[7]

At this state, particles do not have mass yet. A particle's rest-energy results in the particle having mass through the agency of a Higgs Boson.[4,13,16] Guth's model of rapid inflation states that the energy of the electromagnetic field is concentrated in bundles of photons. This is similar to how the energy of the electron field is concentrated in bundles of electrons. Every particle is described as a bundle of energy in a field.

The Higgs Field has nonzero values that are similar to a charge, permeating the vacuum of space. Since the particles in a field always settle into a state of the lowest possible energy density, the Higgs Mechanism of spontaneous broken symmetry gives gravitational energy to an object proportional to the Higgs Field.[7] This means that energy in the form of particles acquires mass once they interact with the Higgs field via a Higgs Boson. No mass can exist and photons would dominate in an early universe in which the temperature exceeds the Higgs value.[4] Therefore, with the Higgs Mechanism, it is now possible for elementary particles to form and attract each other as the early universe cools.

The Matter Epoch

After 100 seconds, the temperature has dropped to 1 billion degrees. That is about as hot as some of today's hottest stars. Protons and neutrons start to collide and form the basic atom nuclei of deuterium, also known as heavy water, that consists of one proton and one neutron. This is the predominant type of matter formed at this point. This process is followed with production of helium nuclei and small amounts of lithium and beryllium. Remaining neutrons in this primordial soup decayed to protons.[1]

A few hours after the Big Bang's rapid inflation, the production of helium and other atoms stopped while the universe continued expanding for the next million years. The energy possessed by electrons and atoms' nuclei decreased when the universe expanded enough for the temperature to drop to a few thousand degrees. This decrease is significant because atoms start to form when its energy is below that of electromagnetism.[1] The radiation-dominated epoch then gave way to the matter-dominated epoch. The energy density of radiation decreases faster than non-relativistic matter such as matter and baryons.[9]

The Formation of Galaxies (The Hand of God, Part 2)

The universe continued expanding and cooling until it began to structure itself with some regions slightly more dense than others. This effect caused some regional expansion to slow down, and regions eventually started collapsing in on themselves. Matter outside of a collapsing region starts rotating around it and accelerating due to gravitational forces. As each region gets smaller, galaxies start forming.[1]

While matter is collapsing in regions to form galaxies, hydrogen and helium gas in smaller clouds subsequently collapse and contract. This causes the local temperatures to increase. Stars are born when temperatures increase enough to start a nuclear fusion reaction. Fusion produces more helium and some amounts of carbon and oxygen. A star might have a supernova explosion if enough carbon and oxygen form, causing the star's center to collapse. The resulting supernova blows the heavier elements out into the galaxy. These elements become part of the next generation of stars. When these secondary stars formed, the gas clouds around them that contained heavier elements would eventually form the planets and moons in their solar systems.[1]

Regions of gravity with values stronger than that of the expansion of the universe caused galaxies to gravitate towards each other into clumps throughout the universe. This concept, known as regional attraction, led to the making of galaxy clusters. A galaxy cluster is a huge group of galaxies within an area of regional attraction. The universe was Dark Matter-dominated when galaxy clusters and galaxies were forming.[9]

The COBE, WMAP, and Planck measured temperature anomalies from the Big Bang occurred on the last scattering surface when electrons were trapped to form hydrogen atoms in the beginning of the matter-dominated epoch (about 380,000 years). The WMAP data showed that the early universe consisted of 63% Dark Matter and 25% radiation (split into 15% photons and 10% neutrinos). The remainder of this early universe (13%) was Dark Energy. This portion of Dark Energy is much less than the amount of today's approximate estimates of about 70%. Dark Energy may affect post-expansion as well as structure formation. Additionally, it is thought that Dark Energy during the matter-dominated epoch was somehow suppressed to allow for structure formation within the universe.[9]

The Dark Energy Epoch

After the matter-dominated epoch completed the Decoupling, or Dark Energy epoch began, in which Dark Energy dominated the energy of the universe. In the beginning of the Dark Energy epoch, photons were able to move freely without scattering.[9] The Dark Energy epoch is the modern epoch in which we find ourselves in the present time. The Dark Energy epoch is characterized by the discovery that the expansion of the universe is accelerating. This accelerating expansion started about seven billion years ago. This epoch is expected to last until the universe has aged approximately 150 billion years and everything as we know it becomes supercooled as all of the energy is dissipated. This later state is called the Big Freeze.[10]

In summation, our current understanding of the Inflationary Big Bang model of the universe is as follows. There are four main epochs of the Inflationary Big Bang Model: Inflation, Radiation, Matter, and Dark Energy.[9] The Big Bang Inflation occurred first with a faster-than-light expansion of empty space. The beginning of our four-dimensional brane occurred in a bubble within the larger vacuum. Time zero was 13.82 billion years ago, when the radiation epoch began. According to M-Theory, our universe is one of many possible universes in a multi-dimensional space that is known as hyperspace. The production of matter began within a few hours and an expansion that is known as Dark Energy occurred after the initial inflation. The expansion has continued until the current day and time. Moreover, our current model predicts that this expansion will continue for the next 150 billion years because we have observed this accelerating expansion to be irreversible.[10]

Pre-Big Bang Proposals

As I ask in the subtitle of this book, what happened before the Big Bang occurred? If this infinitely hot and dense massless point particle that is only a Planck in length existed in a state wherein the laws of physics break down and the Big Bang occurred, how is it possible for such a particle to be in that state in the first place? In 2010, Sir Roger Penrose published a pre-Big Bang proposal in which a mirror image of the Big Bang loops at the point where expansion takes over. This ever-expanding cycle is known as conformal cyclic cosmology (CCC).[4]

I also have a proposal, though it differs from Penrose's and others discussed in his book.[4] In the next chapters, we will discuss the concept and feasibility regarding my proposal, known as the Grand Slam Theory of the Omniverse. Prepare yourself. What you are about to learn will change how you view the universe.

THE OMNIVERSE CONCEPT

"When the solution is simple, God is answering."
—Albert Einstein

The Grand Slam Theory describes a scenario of what could have happened before the Big Bang. We look at the origin of the Big Bang and attempt to describe why it was not stable at time zero, when the Big Bang occurred. However, it must have been stable in some form before the Big Bang in order for the singularity to have existed in the first place, until something changed. This one dilemma is the basis for proposing what happened before time zero. The beauty of the Grand Slam is its simplicity.

The origin of the Big Bang particle can be represented with a simplified, scalable diagram small enough to be written on a sticky note. Figure 5 shows the graphical concept of the proposed Omniverse Model. It is essentially the same as the simplified version on the inside cover of the book.

With this model, we can address two basic unanswered questions of the universe:

1) What caused the initial inflation?
2) What could have initialized the unknown antigravity force causing expansion?
   Let's see how.

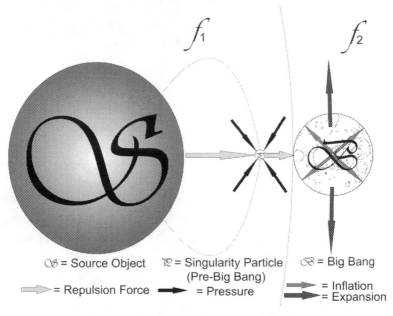

f_1 f_2

$\mathcal{OS}$ = Source Object $\mathcal{P}$ = Singularity Particle $\mathcal{B}$ = Big Bang
(Pre-Big Bang)
= Repulsion Force   = Pressure   = Inflation
= Expansion

Figure 5: The Proposed Omniverse Model: The Omniverse involves a singularity particle's source and field interactions allowing the singularity to become the Inflationary Big Bang.

This diagram represents the progression of the Big Bang particle ($\mathcal{P}$) that comes from the source area ($\mathcal{OS}$) within the primary field (f_1). It is important to realize that pressure energies within this field, denoted by arrows, are greater than or equal to the energy of the universe. Therefore, the particle is stable. In addition to the primary energy conceptually represented by pressure, there is one other principal energy of motion that is being fueled by repulsive forces (wide arrows). This energy must be greater than the energy of the primary field for the particle to escape. This means that the source of the particle must imprint it with enough energy to be released from the grip the source has on the pre-Big Bang particle. This source does this with repulsive force. Therefore, the particle has repulsive force and is under an intense amount of pressure-like energy before the Big Bang occurs. This is the energy required to make the singularity stable before the Big Bang starts at time zero.

For the singularity, or point particle that started the Big Bang ($\oslash$), we know that it would have to be unstable in order for the post-Big Bang universe to exist. The particle has to contain a great amount of internal energy in order for the Big Bang to 1) initiate itself and 2) progress through its final expansion epoch. Now that the particle enters the second and lower energy field (f_2), it becomes the Inflationary Big Bang as we know it. In addition, Einstein's Classical Theory holds true within the circle representing the Big Bang. This is the initial "bubble" universe that we described in the Inflationary Big Bang Model. Thus, we now have a source of energy required to initiate the Big Bang.

The Grand Slam Theory of the Omniverse

Imagine the baseball from our grand slam scenario that was hit out of the ballpark. Recall how it sailed past the stands, out of the stadium, and finally crashed outside the ballpark? Let's suppose that the ball falls into a body of icy water. Furthermore, let's suppose that the ball is white-hot, as was the universe during the early stages of the Big Bang. The first thing that you would see as the ball splashes into the water is the ripples that result from the impact. This white-hot ball, now submerged in water, begins to interact with its new surroundings. As ripples fly away in concentric circles on the above surface at an alarming rate, the heat dissipates in the water with an expanding radius of increasing temperature.

In the middle of all the dissipating pressure waves and heat, the submerged ball is still very hot after having been in the water for only a short amount of time. The ball is so hot that it makes the water boil around it. Suppose that the underwater bubbles do not just float away. These ones stay beneath the surface and start to attract each other. Smaller bubbles combine into larger bubbles. The conglomerate bubble spreads out while following the surface of the water but remaining submerged. This results in a bubble that appears to be flattening out just beneath the surface, as if the surface was frozen over. Think you've never seen a bubble do that? As it turns out, we live in one. It is our universe.

Let's compare the hot baseball bubble to our current universe. Instead of throwing a baseball into a body of water, we are going to hurl a singularity – the pre-Big Bang particle – into a field that acts like the fluid. We do know that according to the Big Bang Theory, this singularity was indeed white-hot because it was full of energy in the form of heat at the time the Big Bang occurred. There was so much energy that it was not stable enough to maintain itself in that state, according to the Big Bang Theory. It just couldn't hold itself in!

So how do we go from just unstable to actually forming the Inflationary Big Bang? The Omniverse model proposes that the pre-Big Bang singularity originates from the source object and contains energies represented as pressure and repulsion. Repulsion is responsible for the pathway of the singularity, or point particle, away from the source while the pressure maintains its stability in the primary high-energy field. In essence, it is an energy transfer from one field to another outlying field, like the ball being hit out of the ballpark.

With another analogy, let us visualize ourselves watching the pathway of the singularity particle being pulled from the source. Take a look at a solar flare as an example. The pathway of a singularity might look a lot like a solar flare flying from the surface of the Sun while exhibiting properties of both particles and waves. We have all seen pictures of solar flares on the surface of the sun. They look like giant waves of energy. In fact, they are huge amounts of electromagnetic energy.

Scientists have been studying how and why solar flares can become Coronal Mass Ejections, or CMEs, that as the name suggests result in matter being ejected away from the sun and its gravitational influence. Figure 6 presents a graphical image of solar flares emitted from the surface of the sun that could produce a coronal mass ejection. This is what such phenomena might look like when the source object ejects a pre-Big Bang particle. In the Omniverse model, it's not matter that is ejected, but a singularity consisting of infinite energy.

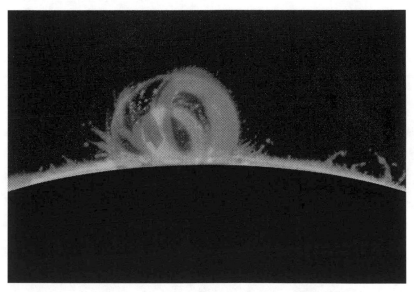

Figure 6: Solar Flare Producing a Coronal Mass Ejection
The Omniverse's source field and pre-Big Bang singularity may resemble a solar flare producing a coronal mass ejection. Copyright: Photodisc 2013

Occasionally, we have witnessed spectacular solar flares in which the sun outputs great amounts of energy in the form of light and radiation. These can travel as far as Earth and beyond, and sometimes they disrupt our satellites as they pass through the upper atmosphere. Similar to how the Standard Model of physics describes everything as particles, we can compare the singularity to a particle with energies giving it the properties of a solar flare or similar mechanism. This flare repels the pre-Big Bang particle away from the source similar to the sun producing a coronal mass ejection, and this is when the magic happens.

When the particle is far enough from the source to be out of the influence of the primary high-energy field, it begins to enter the lower energy secondary field (f_2). And it does this with a splash! Like the ball landing in water, it actually leaves measurable ripples in space along the boundary. No longer affected by the immense pressure energy of the primary field, its internal energy is now greater than its surroundings. Therefore, we are going from a state of higher energy to a state of lower energy in the secondary field, similar to the pencil that fell and broke symmetry in the demonstration of the Higgs mechanism.

This splash gives way to the inflation of the universe when the particle enters the secondary field and releases its internal energy. The burst of internal energy results in the initial inflation of the universe as the bubbles formed from the white-hot singularity become submerged in the fluid-like field. This is like when the white-hot ball entered the water. Therefore, the pre-Big Bang particle's initial energy can be related to a pressure-like energy that held the particle stable via the mechanism of the primary field. This resulted in the inflationary universe, but the singularity still has its repulsive force energy stored inside it, and now its leftover energy manifests itself as expansion.

As the conglomerate bubble formed just below the surface, we tend to observe a flattening of our universe. The ongoing influx of repulsive energy results in continued expansion of this bubble that formed as it became one with other bubbles and spread out. This process formed the universe into what it is currently observed. Therefore, repulsion is the force responsible for continued expansion of the universe, and it comes from the source object in the Omniverse model.

Now that the pre-Big Bang particle has interacted with the second lower energy field, it has become the Inflationary Big Bang exactly as we know it. Moreover, our Big Bang – our entire universe – is sitting outside of the source area and primary field, giving us a much bigger view of our universe. Further evidence supporting this is the fact that we have found our universe to be finite. It has boundaries in all directions from us and is not continuous as once thought. Previously, we had no idea if anything existed outside the universe. This proposal adds to our current understanding of the finite universe. This is the concept of the Omniverse.

The Big Bang is a singularity – a point particle – that comes from a source object and primary field, moves to another lower-energy state of existence and becomes part of a second field where the Inflationary Big Bang is able to occur. The state of the singularity is the point at which "the laws of physics break down" because they are conceived when time starts at the Big Bang! So in summation, the universe occurs at the boundary of the field around the source object, which is the basic foundation of the model of the Omniverse.

Where else in nature do we see a field around an object? We know objects like planets and stars have electromagnetic fields where energies are carried. In addition, we have the current model of the atom with its electron field. Electrons aren't just particles that orbit a nucleus. They are much more than that. Electrons are actually a field around the nucleus that can exist in multiple states of excitement that determine the field's energy and distance from the nucleus.

What the basic model of the Omniverse looks like is a larger version of a simple atom with one electron that exists in two states, or two fields. I believe that in order to apply knowledge outside of our known universe and predict the structure of the Omniverse, we can observe how objects interact within our universe. This can be viewed as a basic repeating pattern of the universe that is much like a fractal version of itself. The Omniverse is a fractal atom and the universe is its electron field!

A Simplified Mathematical Approach

Without going deep into calculations at this point, I would like to propose a simplified approach by using the amounts of known energies that we know must exist in order to balance out the universe. A basic input/output equation can be used. Basically, the universe consists of matter and energy (5%), dark matter (27%), and dark energy (68%). The sum of these is the total energy level that the singularity has when time begins. Although the ratios have changed during the formation of the universe, they always add up to 100%, or 1. Since energy is neither created nor destroyed, this value will always be the same.

This mathematical approach is borrowed from the hydrological equation that balances inflows and outflows. Call it hydrology of the universe if you will. The total volume of a hydrologic system is equal to the total of its precipitation, evaporation, runoff, and overflow. Apply this model to the universe's total energies and you would have something similar. The total sum of energies in a fundamental

Omniverse Model is equal to the sum of its universe's matter, forces, dark matter, and dark energy.

Mathematically, this translates to:

$$E = m + f + m_d + e_d$$

where:

m = matter

f = force

m_d = dark matter

e_d = dark energy

and E = total system energy (after the Big Bang in this case)

Because the pre-Big Bang singularity particle was under two kinds of energy, pressure and repulsive force, E is also equal to the sum of these two.

$$E = e_p + e_r$$

where:

e_p = energy of pressure

e_r = energy of repulsion

and E = total system energy (before the Big Bang in this case)

This tells us that the sum of matter, forces, dark matter, and dark energy are equal to the sum of pressure and repulsive energies before the Big Bang started. This state is actually the criteria necessary for the Big Bang to happen. However, these two sides will vary if we apply the principle of sum over histories. We just happen to exist in the most likely quantum probability, thus allowing us to exist!

This is where the fields come into the picture. We will not delve into the deep mathematics of Quantum Field Theory, but we can generalize information. If the energies of the primary field are equal to or greater than the secondary field then we would have something similar to a coronal mass ejection, or the excited state of an electron field.

$$f_1 \geq f_2,$$

Therefore, in this scenario we have the Big Bang happening at time zero. However, we can't predict what actually happens if there is a large discrepancy. The Big Bang might be more powerful and result in a universe with different laws, or even no universe at all.

Conversely, where $f_1 < f_2,$

The particle is just a particle without being able to escape the source and no Big Bang occurs. As you can see, there are many possibilities that can result in failed universes and an unknown amount of quantum possibilities for a single universe to form.

Since this equation favors the primary field being stronger than the secondary field, this requires an energy input into the singularity particle that is stabilized within the primary field. This causes an energy rebound when the field is no longer strong enough to hold the particle within itself, thus resulting in inflation and expansion via pressure and repulsive forces.

Decay and the Measurement of Time

As the particle in motion travels beyond the outer reach of the first primary field's stronger energy and enters the weaker secondary field, it goes from a higher energy state to a lower state. It breaks symmetry and releases its primary energy (e_p, the pressure energy that allowed the particle to remain stable in imaginary time) in the form of the rapid expansion of the universe (inflation) where subatomic particles, weak and strong energies, and fields are created systematically in the reaction and decay with time. Thus, time is a measurement of decay.

The Inflationary Big Bang has been well documented as a reaction marking the inception of the universe from the moment when time began, and most scientific evidence has supported the theory. Matter and energies known to mankind existed upon the initiation of the Big Bang, and time is used to measure their decay. However, time does not exist without the presence of the universe in the state of constant decay that we observe and measure. This makes the equation essentially free of time constraints. Therefore, in the Omniverse model, we are looking at "imaginary" time that is the decay of a larger system before the Big Bang.

Events that lead up to time zero must take place in this imaginary time that is also viewed as "backwards" time. By cancelling out time and imaginary time in order to include the "full picture," the Omniverse is not just a reaction that occurs with time such as the Big Bang. The source, the particle, and the energies involved on both sides exist across all measured and imaginary time. We could call this the quantum probability of time. If any state of decay exists, it can be measured to any time in a system. Additionally, all states of decay, thus all states of time exist within the sum of histories. Thus, time as we think of it does not really exist whereas *all* of time does. All of the information contained in all states of decay must exist. In other words, past, present, future, and imaginary time exist within the system. All time exists in the universe.

A Universe without Time

If time is cancelled outside of our universe, then the source can be viewed as a constant that is similar to the cosmological constant. The first primary pressure energy is equal to the initial inflation of the universe because such energy is propelled by the energy that created it. The second repulsion energy that is still present in the universe is the motion that translates to the spreading or expansion of the current universe. What this suggests is that the entire universe is in a state of energy transfer or motion in imaginary time with each and every part of the universe equal to that energy. Therefore, if the universe as a whole is moving in one direction or experiencing an energy transfer equally, it would not be able to be observed by red shift that is used to measure the motion of the universe relative to other parts of the universe. There would be no change in momentum for any particle that was not equal to the same change in momentum in another particle.

With the universe in motion before the Big Bang, a second field is encountered that may absorb the energy of the motion as energies fall to a lower state. This is the splash of the ball, or the singularity, as it leaves the primary field and enters the secondary fluid-like field of lower energy. This transfer of energy creates a flattening and widening of the universe. Thus, expansion occurs. Expansion can be observed throughout the universe, and it seems to be accelerating in the outermost edges of the universe where an event horizon is encountered. This event horizon is similar to that of a black hole in which objects are being pulled into the hole. However, the contents of the universe are accelerated outward to a point where objects can never come back. Essentially, this event horizon is a point of no return where matter and energies cannot escape it. Objects are literally pulled out of the universe, according to our current view. It almost sounds like the old belief of the flat Earth, where one might fall off the edge of the planet if one sailed too far.

Repeating Patterns

The diagram at the beginning of this chapter represents this basic process that can be repeated. As discussed, the Omniverse resembles an atom on a different scale. The universe is like the electron field that occurs around the nucleus. Atoms bond together to form molecules. Molecules become the building blocks of a crystal lattice that repeats itself. Thus, these basic patterns create repeating units. We see repeating units and patterns when we view the interactions in the Omniverse model. The basic properties of the motion or energy transfer of the singularity particle within the first primary field are mimicked by every individual subatomic particle within the Inflationary Big Bang universe that was created by this singularity. What this means is that atoms are formed in a way that mimics the Omniverse. They are created in its image, so to speak.

Another important observation of repeating units that can be made within our solar system is that of the "Ring of Life" or the "Goldilocks Zone." For example, we observe that life in our solar system forms in a relatively narrow zone that is between the principle gravitational object of the sun and the secondary gravitational object of Jupiter. Venus, Earth, and Mars lie within this zone. However, Earth is in the orbit with the strongest life force, thus facilitating the inception and evolution of biological life. A similar pattern can also be observed in the Milky Way galaxy. With the areas around the galaxy's central supermassive black hole, there are regions close to it that are consumed, and there are regions close enough not to be pulled into the black hole, yet a safe distance from the outer edges of the galaxy.

The habitable zone of the Omniverse model is exactly where the Inflationary Big Bang exists! This is the region where the singularity results in the Inflationary Big Bang. This is the grand slam!

The key to recognizing this process of repeating units is to observe the repetitions of small sized quantum scale particles in the universe and the larger objects within it such as atoms, solar systems, and galaxies. For the purposes of discussing the origin of the Big Bang, this scalar repeating pattern is viewed as the Omniverse. The pre-Big Bang singularity exists without the presence of time, because all states of decay exist. Therefore, there is no beginning and no end to this ongoing process.

The Take Away

The main points addressed in this section discuss the "big picture" view of the Omniverse. It creates a singularity, resulting in the Inflationary Big Bang, and then the universe and its components decay in measurable time. Time, however, has no consequences in the big picture approach because every quantum possibility of the universe can exist. Our present is simply the most likely combination of all possibilities that exist.

The Omniverse model may be tested by comparing the model to repeating patterns of the universe. The Omniverse model has similarities to other known attributes of the universe ranging from subatomic particles to large scale structures. Next, we will go into more detail and compare the Omniverse model to all of the modern physics theories about the universe that we discussed in Chapter 3 to see if it is compatible. By comparing, we hope to find verification that this model exists in nature, determine if it needs to be modified, find other ways in which it can be tested, and ultimately determine how to observe and measure the phenomena.

THE GRAND SLAM THEORY OF THE OMNIVERSE EXPLAINED

"In you is such a Beauty and a Power and a Love that
can never die. Life is good, can you feel it?"
—Michael Bernard Beckwith

In 2010, Hawking and Mlodinow wrote that physics is making a model-dependent realism that is based upon the idea that our brains actually interpret the sensory input by making a model of the world we observe.[8] Such a model-dependent realism would allow us to provide a framework to discuss what happened before the Big Bang. This model should include the following:

1. It should be elegant
2. It must contain only a few arbitrary or adjustable arguments
3. It should agree with and explain all existing observations
4. It should make detailed predictions about future observations that can ultimately disqualify the model if predictions cannot be observed.[8]

As we saw in the last chapter, the Omniverse model is quite simple and elegant. Without being a complex mathematical formula, it sets the framework for a much-larger-than-Big-Bang universe. The framework of the proposed Omniverse model is based on a simple geometric principle, as shown in the previous section.

It only contains a few arguments and variabilities that include a source object, a singularity (the pre-Big Bang point particle), fundamental energies (pressure and repulsion), and two fields. When the particle undergoes repulsive force, it travels from the source until its primary field is not strong enough to keep it stable anymore. It reaches a secondary field where it falls to a lower state of energy resulting in rapid inflation and continued expansion using the same Inflationary Big Bang model we have today.

The third argument that it should agree with all known observations is also true. To show this, we will compare the Omniverse Model with the major accomplishments of physics that were summarized in Chapter 3. While most of the research we will be comparing the model to will be from the 20th and 21st century, we should first consider Newton's laws of physics.

The Laws of Physics

Newton's laws of physics are crucial to a physical model. I questioned the Big Bang Theory by first looking to the laws of physics to provide an explanation for the fact that the pre-Big Bang was unstable. This instability resulted in the rapid inflation that started the creation of our universe. My question was simple. How did it exist in the first place if it was not stable? I believe the Omniverse model answers this question, and we will put it to the test. Let us start with the first law of physics.

Newton's 1st law of conservation of energy states that a body in motion is affected by a force that changes the speed of the body versus the force that set it in motion. When a body is not acted on by any force (i.e. friction), it keeps on moving.[3] In such a case, the model does compare to a moving object. The pre-Big Bang singularity particle is affected by forces of pressure and repulsion that set it in motion. When it encounters a change in force, it keeps moving by spreading outward. This model appears to be consistent with Newton's 1st law.

Newton's 2nd law of motion predicts that acceleration due to gravity is always the same, proportional to the object's mass. Therefore, twice the weight of an object equals twice the gravity and twice the mass.[3] In the Inflationary Big Bang model, mass is attributed to particles via the Higgs Mechanism after the inflationary and radiation epochs. Thus, this physical law does not apply to a pre-Big Bang scenario because nothing had mass until after the Big Bang started. Remember that we may be dealing with higher dimensions in which our laws of physics may or may not apply. In the case of what happened before the Big Bang, Newton's 2nd law does not apply yet. However, the Omniverse model can be consistent with the law because the model incorporates the post-Inflationary Big Bang scenario. After the Big Bang, no changes are proposed by the Omniverse model, thus Newton's 2nd law applies to our universe only.

Another way to compare to the 2nd law, since mass didn't exist in the pre-Big Bang era, is to look at entropy. As noted previously, entropy is always greater later rather than earlier in a system. Entropy means that nature tends to move from order to disorder in isolated systems. Entropy appeared to have reached a minimum rather than a maximum at the beginning of the Big Bang.[4] However, Penrose showed it was consistent with the 2nd law. With nearly uniform cosmic background radiation, entropy was low at the beginning. Quantum fluctuations in radiation correlated to the formation of galaxies. Therefore, entropy was always increasing.[4]

The question is do we see our Omniverse model starting with less entropy than the beginning of the Big Bang? The model starts with a source object that gives rise to a point particle and then sends the particle on a journey where it experiences the process of rapid inflation, continued expansion, and everything that is known about the Inflationary Big Bang model. This appears to be consistent with a system of increasing entropy.

Newton's 3rd law of force asserts that when two bodies interact by exerting force on one another, the forces of action and reaction are equal in magnitude but opposite in direction.[3] What this means is that the system needs to be balanced. Pressure and repulsion forces in the pre-Big Bang era were shown to translate into inflation and expansion after the Big Bang. The truth is in the details of complex mathematics that balance the formula, so this math will ultimately need to be tested. In addition, a complete model needs to incorporate gravity. This is because gravity wells in our universe, for example, black holes may actually communicate information back into the Omniverse via a higher-dimensional pathway. This communication may be one possible way of balancing the repulsive forces in our universe that are known as Dark Energy. This may hold consistent if higher-dimensional theories of gravity leakage to higher dimensions are found to be valid. Because the Omniverse model involves higher dimensions, it is feasible.

This model thus agrees with all three of Newton's laws of motion. Now let us take the next step. The model should ultimately be tested mathematically to form hypotheses and test them. However, for the purposes of proposing the idea, we will keep moving on and review how the Omniverse model works with other major accomplishments of physics. The purpose of this book is to present the model but not to put it through more rigorous tests yet. However, I encourage testing the model mathematically with regard to Newton's principles for those interested in further studies. We'll move forward with Einstein's General Relativity.

Classical Theory and the Inflationary Big Bang

Before ever putting this model down on paper or even attempting to write a book about it, I had a great question in my mind. Does the Omniverse model work with Classical Theory? I understand that General Relativity concepts have limitations, especially concerning infinities such as a singularity. The two most common singularities are black holes and the Big Bang. Essentially, Classical Theory does not work when it is outside of what we would consider "normal" space and time. But does that mean that the Omniverse model will conflict with Classical Theory?

The Omniverse model describes physical characteristics outside of and within normal space-time. Einstein's Special and General Relativity would only apply to the part of the Omniverse model that occurs after the Big Bang. In other words, this model changes nothing with respect to Classical Theory. Within four-dimensional space-time, the energy of a system still equals the mass times the speed of light squared ($E=mc^2$).[6] There is no need to rewrite or amend any previous work in Classical Theory as a result of the Omniverse model.

It should be noted that the most recent modification to the current theory regarding the Inflationary Big Bang uses advanced quantum physics to determine the same fundamental thing. Classical Theory cannot work in the pre-Inflationary Big Bang epoch. Recall, however, that the early universe starts to form in bubbles of normal space in the Inflationary Big Bang Model. These bubbles were small at first, then combined to form a larger bubble in which our current laws of physics apply.[7] The quantum physics used to describe the inside of the bubbles remain consistent with Classical Theory. In other words, when the early universe formed inside four-dimensional bubbles, General Relativity reigned, just as it still does.

Thus, we are presented with the argument that Classical Theory can only exist within the post-Big Bang that is just a portion of the Omniverse model. Light and particles with mass all formed after the Big Bang, and these are the main factors in $E=mc^2$. This opens possibilities for the physics that exist outside of our bubble. The speed of light only applies inside the bubble because mass and light only exist in the bubble. The initial inflation at the beginning of the Big Bang expanded space at a rate much faster than light. We no longer have this speed limit outside of our universe. Thus, the speed of space is greater than the speed of light.

Einstein found that information could go faster than light. The EPR experiment showed that information can be exchanged instantaneously.[18] Guth's Inflationary Big Bang showed us that space is a form of information that travels faster than light.[7] Only the photons that form inside the bubbles travel the speed of light. The information contained within inflationary space is all instantaneous in the Omniverse model. This is because the singularity is described as a single particle. That single particle is the Big Bang. The concept of entanglement from the EPR experiments is consistent with this model because all of the individual components of particles, forces, and energies in our universe are still a part of one singular particle. Every atom within all of us is one with the universe. Thus, all atoms are entangled within the universe.

What does entanglement tell us? Every particle is entangled and can transmit information in space faster than light. This property does not have to exist only in the bubble of the Big Bang. In fact, we can show that the Big Bang particle is entangled with its source if we follow this property with the Omniverse mechanism. Entanglement is definitely a subject worthy of further studies in the hope that science can come to a better understanding of its potential. We are currently using it to transmit and teleport particle properties across distances of several miles! Some experiments are underway to test quantum teleportation from the International Space Station. The Omniverse sets a very basic premise regarding how entanglement happens because the Big Bang is a single particle. It does not lose the property of a particle. Thus, it does not lose any information.

Further studies in this field could be done to support the Omniverse model. Quantum Information Theory is being used to describe the transfer of information as matter encounters the event horizon of a black hole. Perhaps further studies would shed light on a similar mechanism in the event horizon of the Omniverse model – when the pre-Big Bang point particle becomes the universe.

I think generally that most people who see this concept for the first time might be in a state of disbelief about it. After all, it is not taught in most science classes. Nevertheless, it happened. It was later repeated, tested, and verified. This has been done several times. Entanglement is real. Information travels faster than light. Therefore, the EPR experiment is a good example to explain how the universe acts as a single particle with all of its components entangled when describing the Omniverse model. Furthermore, the Omniverse contains a source from which this particle originates. Therefore, the Omniverse is also in a state of entanglement. Entanglement is basically a connection of everything, and a connection can exchange information. Thus, information from the source directly affects information in the universe and does so instantly.

There is still more to Classical Theory. The EPR experiment isn't the only thing that they don't teach in most science classes. There is also the letter to Einstein from Kaluza that I just happened to come across after finishing my background research for this book. Kaluza was able to show Einstein's General Relativity by using a five dimensional cylinder. Einstein considered it and rewrote his own work two years later. However, his own paper had negative results. This displeased him. He did not like it because it had no solution that was:

1) Non-singular,
2) Static, and
3) Exactly spherically symmetric.

Einstein may have taken a better look at this if there was a different way to view Kaluza's five dimensions. Now, there is. The Omniverse particle results in every possibility existing at once when Feynman's sum over histories is applied. Thus, it is non-singular. Einstein would not have liked this idea because he was opposed to quantum physics. Nonetheless, it is non-singular. The universe is not static. This has been verified with observational data. I do not see why the universe would have been assumed to be static in the first place. It is just a mathematical assumption that is not supported by evidence. Furthermore, is the universe's symmetry uniform and is it shaped like a sphere? We have seen from recent observations and discoveries that the universe is nearly uniform. Observed cosmic microwave background was nearly the same in all directions on space, when viewed on a large scale. Additionally, we have also observed a flattening effect of the universe related to its expansion. However, this flattened universe unfolds itself, resulting in a sphere when you remove or subtract the 5th dimension.

For example, consider an ordinary globe. It is nearly spherical and symmetrical and can spin it on its axis. It remains uniformly round with only minor variations on the surface that one can feel when they let their fingers gently rub the surface as it spins. This is known as elevation or the 3rd dimension. The first two dimensions are curved east to west and north to south around the surface of the globe. We can take this three-dimensional object and transform it into five dimensions. This is much like projecting the globe to a two-dimensional map. However, this causes distortions when it is projected to a flat two-dimensional surface because the surface's dimensions are curved around the globe. Notice how the two-dimensional map shown in Figure 7 is curved more towards the edges. In addition, our two-dimensional globe actually makes

Antarctica look flattened and stretched out due to this distorted projection. Therefore, when transforming an object such as our globe from its three-dimensional state, we see curvature or distortions on the map in two dimensions.

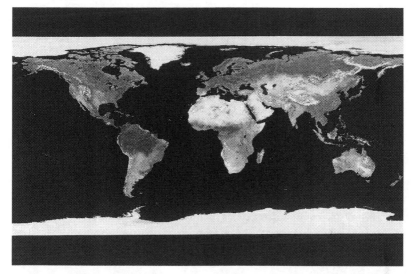

Figure 7 Two-Dimensional Projection of the Earth: The globe in three dimensions appears distorted when plotted along only two dimensions. Copyright: Digital Vision, 2013

Next, we will look at what it looks like when you reverse this to expand the number of dimensions. To do this, we need to collapse three of our dimensions into two as we described. Let's start with a spherical universe and collapse it until it is near flat, like flattening a ball. The first and second boxes in Figure 8 below show this process. In the third box, we can add another dimension of space by putting our flattened universe onto another two-dimensional surface of a sphere. This also adds curvature of the flattened universe.

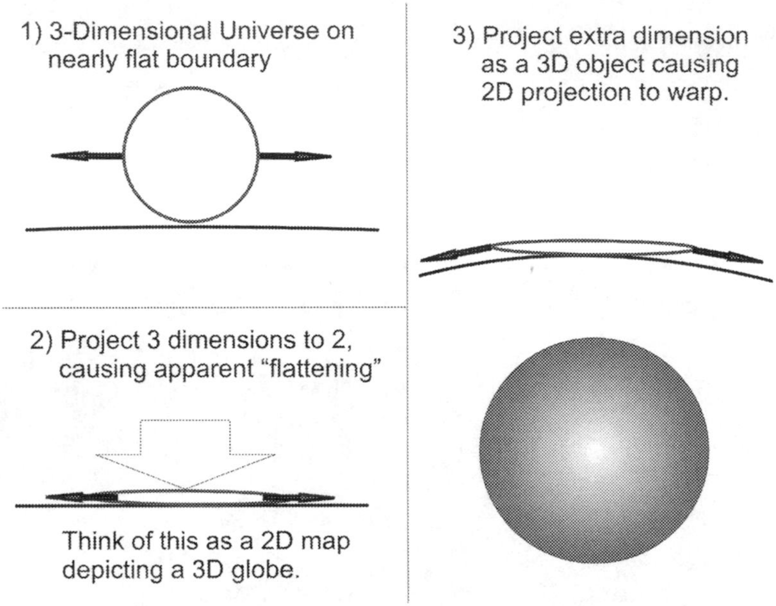

1) 3-Dimensional Universe on nearly flat boundary

2) Project 3 dimensions to 2, causing apparent "flattening"

Think of this as a 2D map depicting a 3D globe.

3) Project extra dimension as a 3D object causing 2D projection to warp.

Figure 8 Projecting a 3-Dimensional Model to 5 Dimensions: Demonstrates how to project a three-dimensional object onto a 5-dimensional surface.

The Omniverse uses this principle of geometry just described. The surface that our three dimensions of space are translated to is the boundary between the two fields. It also has a very unique feature of curvature because this model includes a spherical object outside of the universe's three dimensions of space. Is this consistent with today's flattened universe? This can be tested. We will look at this in more detail later. What we can say at this point is that the five-dimensional geometry is consistent with the universe being spherical in three dimensions. The Omniverse model does remain consistent with a model that includes the attributes of a flattened universe. In fact, this appears to describe flattening quite nicely. Thus, we can show that a spherical object in five dimensions appears flattened as it does with our current Big Bang model. Moreover, it is spherically symmetric in three dimensions of space as Einstein predicted.

Let's sum up how the Omniverse model stacks up to Classical Theory. It is consistent with General Relativity because it needs no alterations to our current knowledge of the subject. General Relativity works in the bubbles that form the space in our universe. The Omniverse also includes a "bubble" that contains the entire universe. In addition, we show how everything in and above this particle is intimately entangled by showing the simplest pathway of a single particle. Space is faster than light and carries information, and information is instantaneous. Finally, the modifications to Einstein's theory in five dimensions help to describe the geometry of the Omniverse model.

Our Omniverse can exist in five dimensions with three space dimensions existing inside the bubbles that form our universe. This is a perfect demonstration of an "ah-ha" moment! Einstein and Guth both observed that the Big Bang model is incomplete. This nearly completes it! Did you say "ah-ha" yet? There's more, so let's explore the next concept.

Quantum Mechanics

In this section, the principles of Quantum Mechanics will be compared to the Omniverse model. These include the uncertainty principle, duality, and Feynman's sum over histories. It appears that the concept of the uncertainty principle may make it difficult for us to accurately observe any phenomena outside of our universe. What the uncertainty principle means is that a quantum particle disturbs another particle in such a way that it cannot be accurately predicted. The more accurately the position of a particle is measured, the less accurate its measure of velocity will be, and vice versa. However, scientists today are finding methods in order to get around this limitation by observing the effects of particles.

The uncertainty principle may have been a setback for making models of a deterministic or predictable universe.[8] However, the Omniverse model uses our observed universe in order to make predictions backwards in time, a concept known as imaginary time. What this ultimately means is that we cannot accurately predict the exact pathway of the pre-Big Bang particle. This is why the Omniverse model is shown in the most simplistic way. The model is a generalization and not meant to be exact. Moreover, all possible properties of that model will exist, as we will see coming up.

Duality means that every particle, wave, and force has its opposite. Here is a way to view this phenomenon in the level of the entire universe. If the universe is expanding, then its antiparticle would be a universe that is simultaneously contracting.[4] What does this mean for the Omniverse proposal? Our entire universe would have an anti-particle. Since we are dealing with the universe on the level of a singularity, its opposite is a black hole. There are attractive forces of gravity in one singularity and in the other type of singularity there is inflation and expansion. For this reason, our Omniverse model can be referred to as a "white hole." This is the opposite of a black hole. It is the superpartner to all of the gravity contained in the universe.

It is possible that the pre-Big Bang singularity point particle and the subsequent Inflationary Big Bang are in fact antiparticles. One particle leads to the Big Bang if we apply chronological time. If we apply negative or imaginary time, we would see the origin of the singularity. In addition, the concept of time is negated by imaginary time. While one might suggest that this would result in a cancellation of the particles, this may help explain why we have duality of particles in the universe. Both the anti-particle and the particle exist without time. This sounds like Hawking's description of virtual particles in which a fundamental particle and its antiparticle cycle back and forth because they exist in all possible states.[8] Next, let's look at why they exist in all possible states.

Recall that Feynman's sum over histories shows us that all possibilities exist when this theory is applied to the singularity particle in the Omniverse model. This is a statistical principle applied to the properties of a particle. Feynman's theory has been thoroughly tested and documented by many of today's brightest physicists. Hawking's latest book described how this principle fits into our Big Bang model and results in parallel universes.[8] Just as within the universe, all possibilities of all particles exist. Moreover, the same principle can be applied to the Omniverse model. This means that all of the quantum possibilities of the singularity particle in my model result in the formation of all possible universes that have their own set of physics. Such a result is what Hawking describes.

In addition to the quantum possibilities of parallel universes, the possibilities of the entire Omniverse model are expanded to the particle's pathway. An imbalance in the energy could have resulted in the pre-Big Bang particle not making it to the secondary field. The Big Bang would not occur in such a scenario, or it could be too powerful and result in subsequent unpredictable levels of excitation such as a "Super Bang." The Big Bang particle can exist in all possible fields. Thus, it can be all possible variations of energy levels. Therefore, the sum of histories theory can apply to the Omniverse model.

The Omniverse model initially appears to be consistent with the basic principles of Quantum Theory regarding the uncertainty principle, duality, and Feynman's sum over histories. In addition,

Hawking published requirements for a new quantum theory and what he believes it should include.[8] Next, let's review what the Omniverse looks like when compared to Hawking's new Quantum Theory requirements:

- It should incorporate Feynman's sum over histories wherein a particle follows every possible path in space-time. Histories should be added up both in real and imaginary time, or a negative value similar to backwards time. Negative time is indistinguishable from directions in space and results in the effective cancellation of space-time. This creates a universe without time.
- Einstein's curved space-time is caused by gravity that is based on Euclidean four-dimensional geometry. This should also incorporate imaginary time.
- In order to make predictions, we must calculate various possibilities.[1]

These points describe how the Omniverse model incorporates Feynman's sum over histories and uses imaginary time. As discussed previously, our Omniverse model describes how all time possibilities exist and effectively cancel chronological time. We also showed that all of space-time is flattening onto a curved surface. This also cancels time because such curvature incorporates both real and negative time. All possibilities thus exist in the past, present, and future. However, the geometric concept of Omniverse model does need to be mathematically verified. Overall, it appears to be a good match for Hawking's quantum theory requirements.

Quantum Field Theories

Now that we appear to be consistent with early quantum theory principles, let's take a look at how our Omniverse model compares to Quantum Field Theories. First, Gauge Theories involve strong and weak interactions and gauge bosons.[12] All gauge reactions occurring in the universe would be unaffected because these fit into the physics of the post-Big Bang era. Second is Supersymmetry. This principle means that properties of a system are unaffected by a transformation such as rotating in space or mirror imaging, excluding transformations of ordinary space.[15] In this sense, force and matter particles are partnered with each other.[8] In the Omniverse model, the Big Bang singularity is like a particle partnered with similar force particles. The force particles are fundamentally the same as the pre-Big Bang singularity as a particle and include pressure and repulsive forces. Moreover, this system does have a transformation of space when the inflation starts in the Big Bang.

What this may result in are different symmetries before and after the Big Bang. The interesting point here is that either side of the system is unaffected by rotations in space with the exception of the Inflationary epoch of the Big Bang. This was the "bang" in the Big Bang and was time-zero. Therefore, there would be no way that the motion of the rotating would affect anything if the entire universe were spinning. If the pre-Big Bang singularity was acting as a particle in motion, it would not have effects in the post-Big Bang universe. Our universe would be unaffected.

Now, we just talked about Supersymmetry and determined that the universe may be symmetric before or after the Big Bang. However, it is not so during the Inflation of the Big Bang at time zero. An important concept involved in the Higgs Mechanism is called broken symmetry.[13,16] We just demonstrated how symmetry can be broken at the point of inception of the Inflationary Big Bang model. The "charge" of the Higgs Field is actually a lower energy state. Thus, it makes the preferred pathway for the interaction. The Omniverse model had two fields. One field has the stronger forces of pressure and repulsion and a second has a lower energy field. This is very similar to the scientific principle of the Higgs Field.

The Standard Model and Higgs Mechanism

We will discuss how this model works with and complements the Higgs field. Even though the Higgs mechanism has been around since the 1960s, I only recently found out about it when beginning to write this book. I had not considered it with the Omniverse model until after the discovery was announced. Then I researched it and found that it supports the model.

So with the Omniverse model, we have a pre-Big Bang particle "falling" toward the Higgs Field. Furthermore, the particle is in a higher state of energy because it is in the primary field. When the particle reaches the secondary field, which could actually be the Higgs Field, the symmetry of the entire universe is broken and it "falls" into a lower state of energy. This is the beginning of the universe, or time-zero. Space as we know it unfolds in an instant without the higher energy state pushing on it with constant pressure. This faster-than-light expansion is the inflation of space that has to happen before the magic begins.

Upon the Big Bang, the universe produces particles which then interact with the Higgs Field that is everywhere in empty space. First, photons are produced. However, they have no mass because they do not interact with the weak force. Then, matter particles start to form and interact with the Higgs Field. When I was a kid and teachers told me that space was empty, it didn't make sense to me. It had to be full of stuff we have not yet discovered, and it is. It would make understanding the universe much simpler if everybody taught this concept. Space is not "nothing." It's everything. It is just pressureless. But on the part of the Omniverse model in imaginary time before the Big Bang, space contains everything and pressure. It contains enough "stuff" to balance our current model of energies in the universe.

So the fields are everywhere, and the Big Bang particle inflates everywhere in an instant when it interacts with the field. A particle of matter acquires mass through the agency of the Higgs Mechanism. According to Randall, a particle's mass can tell us two things: 1) how it responds to forces, and 2) how it travels through space.[13] Thus, we can now read some of the underlying properties of particles such as a particle's resistance to an applied force. Mass gives us this resistance. But did the pre-Big Bang particle respond to forces and travel through space without mass? Is there another mechanism in the stronger primary field that may also result from interaction with that field and affect how it responds to forces and travels through space? There would have to be a mechanism involved that holds the pre-Big Bang particle stable until it reaches the secondary field.

Such a mechanism would most likely impart a particle with another kind of energy because it would not involve mass. What this means is that the pre-Big Bang singularity is interacting with a stronger field that gives it high energy. This high energy produces the Inflationary Big Bang as the energy falls. We know that the pre-Big Bang particle was imparted with huge amounts of energy because it was particle of pure heat. So much that it could not contain itself. There are two basic types of energy as previously mentioned. The immense pressure of the pre-Big Bang particle is acquired by responding to the forces in the stronger primary field. The second type of energy is how the particle travels through space. This is its repulsion. This moves the particle from the primary field to the secondary field as its source pushes the particle away. The secondary field is a lower energy field such as the Higgs Field.

These two energies of pressure and repulsion can be observed in our universe. The pressure of the pre-Big Bang translates into the inflation of the Big Bang. The repulsion provides the fuel necessary to cause the universe to continually expand. Therefore, there must be an underlying mechanism similar to what we have with the Higgs Mechanism. This mechanism would involve a different field that we identified and a basic particle that gives the energy properties to the pre-Big Bang particle. This is the source object of the Omniverse.

So essentially, what I have done is taken a discovery that was announced on July 4th, 2012 and asked even more questions regarding how the process repeats itself on a different level. What is the nature of the other mechanism that happens in a stronger primary field before the universe has started the Big Bang? Are there more levels? If so, how many levels are there? Interestingly, there are some different Higgs models that do include two fields.

The Omniverse model can be tested by applying the principles of the Higgs Mechanism to the stronger primary field. This will describe how the particle falls from a higher to a lower state. The universe particle does go from higher to lower energy states as do all ordinary matter particles. But instead of a Big Bang particle acquiring mass, this primary mechanism involves the singularity acquiring space and energy. Thus, the energy transfer initiated the Inflationary Big Bang. Furthermore, this mechanism keeps fueling the universe's expansion for over 150 billion years.

If we have another mechanism like the Higgs Mechanism, what does this mean for the Standard Model? Should we also be able to predict new particles observable in our universe if we discover new forces? Perhaps we could find signatures of more elementary particles in supercollider experiments that are synonymous with the repulsive and pressure forces known as dark energy and inflation. This remains to be seen, but the Omniverse model gives a direction of where we can go with further studies of the Higgs Boson and the Standard Model. With today's successes of the Standard Model and the Higgs Mechanism, such study would bolster the Omniverse model if force particles that link our universe to inflation and dark energy can be identified.

We may also identify underlying forces. It is thought that all forces are variations of the same underlying force. We identified the four basic forces of gravity, electromagnetic, weak, and strong forces. We are proposing underlying forces of pressure and repulsion representing inflation and dark energy. Understanding the nature of these forces may help us to discover how to predict new forces and then determine ways to test them.

The Fifth Dimension

When Kaluza applied Einstein's equations in five dimensions, what he found was that Maxwell's theory of light was observable via ripples in the fifth dimension that correspond to light waves in four-dimensional space-time. We then learned how to visualize the Omniverse using five dimensions. When we apply Kaluza's description, we see that photons exist only on one side of the boundary between fields. Thus, we live in a universe of light. Photons exist in our universe and its dimensions, but these photons form ripples on the fifth dimension. These ripples are also consistent with the description of the Omniverse. When the particle splashed into the secondary field, it produced ripples similar to the surface of water. Furthermore, this is observable with current studies that were undertaken in order to analyze the cosmic ripples in the early Big Bang.

Another way to test the Omniverse model would be to compare its conceptual five dimensions to gravitational leakage in five dimensions. Gravity's intensity is very weak when compared to the intensity of the other three major forces. This is because the fifth dimension actually attenuates gravity. Thus, gravity is stronger in the higher dimension where other forces also dominate. However, it is weaker than the strong, weak, and electromagnetic forces in our dimensions.[10,16] In the flattened bubble on Figure 8, picture a stronger gravity leaking into the stronger repulsive field. We might find that these two might be superpartners and that gravity may be related to repulsion.

Basically, there would be a give and take reaction when gravity leaks into the higher dimensions. Gravity leaks out of our bubble and repulsion displaces it. Thus, we have a source for expansion that might be measurable. Further study in this field is definitely needed. Balancing repulsion and gravity across dimensions may provide the best evidence for the Omniverse model. The mechanism of the five dimensional gravity leakage used principles of String Theories and M-Theory that we can now use in comparison to the Omniverse model. So let's dive in!

String Theory and White Holes

Don't look back, we're taking the journey of a lifetime. We're going into a black hole. And we might just come out of a white hole. A white hole is a theoretical superpartner with repulsive force to a black hole's massive attraction. Do you see where this is going already? By studying the nature of a singularity, we learn about our universe as a whole.

In String Theory, particles are vibrations of a string or a straw with an infinite length. As we said earlier, String Theory competed with Quantum Field Theory in their descriptions of a string near the event horizon of a black hole.[14] This is the point at which nothing can escape the gravitational force of the singularity. While the Omniverse theory does not change current knowledge of black holes, the event horizon may be a shared feature. Its event horizon becomes the point where nothing can actually go back in if the source generates a strong enough repulsive force.

In a sense, the source becomes the opposite of what we would regard as a black hole that is the size of the universe. However, does this type of event horizon wherein something never goes back in affect anything? Yes, it most certainly does! It appears to be at the border between the primary field and the secondary field. Inflation spread out space in a uniform matter when the Inflationary Big Bang started, but the universe became flattened afterward. We noted earlier that the flattening could be a result of simply viewing it in more than three or four dimensions. This flattening would be occurring on one side of that border that may effectively push back the universe as it flattens. Thus, a mechanism for Dark Energy might not be far off from being discovered.

When we threw a superhot object into water, we described how the water instantly vaporized into bubbles of boiling water. The bubbles coalesced and made bigger bubbles but never again broke through the surface. It would be as if the surface was now covered with ice. The giant bubbles would flatten out just beneath the surface of ice because the smaller ones combined. This is the effect we get with the universe. The boundary between fields or the event horizon of a supermassive white hole is similar to the ice on top of the water.

The bubbles will not go back to the other side. However, they will form larger bubbles and then flatten out near the surface.

So what is on the other side when you encounter the event horizon of a black hole? Susskind states that information stored in the system would spread all over its event horizon. Thus, no information loss occurs. An observer outside the black hole would see an object as a string diffusing over an increasing area. However, the falling object would seem fixed from its viewpoint. Thus, this string would appear to the first observer like an ever-expanding plane propeller spread across the event horizon while the object was diffusing. The observer brave enough to accompany an object falling into a black hole would not see what the first observer saw. In essence, time would slow to a near halt for this observer. In either scenario, the information is not lost.[14]

When the object descends into the black hole, its information is completely disassembled and spread evenly across the event horizon of the black hole. The concept of the white hole is interesting when compared to a black hole. Everything in a white hole would start from a single point particle with zero dimensions, similar to a black hole. The white hole causes repulsive forces to push a daughter particle out. This daughter particle is full of all of the information in the entire universe. It is the entire universe in a smaller package. Upon breaching the white hole's event horizon, the particle inflates thus forming our universe as we know it. The universe then continues expanding exponentially. Information in both scenarios is spread across the event horizon of the object.

How does the Omniverse look when compared to the next version of String Theory? We talked about Superstring Theory before. This abandons the concept that elementary constituents of matter are point particles. Well, I just compared the singularity that existed before the Big Bang as a point particle. On the other hand, this is but one theory incorporated into M-Theory, or the mother of all String Theories. Maybe if we look holistically at M-Theory we will have a better picture of how the Omniverse compares.

M-Theory and Curved Dimensions

While we compared a couple of ideas from String Theory, this model would ultimately need to be tested mathematically by experts in the field. However, we have not yet sought out the most all-encompassing version of the String theories. That version is M-Theory, the mother of all String Theories. M-Theory is also the "mother" of the universe because it also incorporates General Relativity. The beginning of M-Theory was all theoretical mathematics. At its inception in the mid-1990s, M-Theory was conceived by slicing an 11-dimensional model five ways, coinciding with five different String Theories.[15] M-Theory also incorporates Supersymmetry and Supergravity. Thus, we can check the Omniverse model to M-Theory as a whole rather than compare the Omniverse model to every last String Theory.

Recall in our discussion about a top-down approach that M-Theory is described as a top-down model because it starts with mathematics. Therefore, it is incomplete. We have not yet found its bottom that is rooted in geometric principles. Conversely, a bottom-up approach would 1) describe the theory from beginning to end, as does the standard model of physical interaction and 2) use the laws of physics in order to calculate how history develops with time.[8] To start a quantum theory, we usually start by writing down the geometry or symmetry of the theory and then write down the action. The action is used to make predictions about the theory.[15]

Here is a very interesting observation. The Omniverse model starts from the basic geometry. A point particle originates from a source object and the action follows. Repulsion forces the particle out of the primary field and into a Higgs or Higgs-like secondary field. The Inflationary Big Bang is then born and keeps expanding. In the next chapter, we will look for ways to make predictions. The Grand Slam Theory of the Omniverse is a bottom-up model as opposed to the top-down M-Theory version. However, it is similar to M-Theory in that this model is incomplete. This proposal of the Omniverse model incorporates the geometry and the action – the parts missing from M-Theory.

The idea of the Omniverse first came to me in the mid-1990s, approximately the same time that scientists were developing M-Theory. Was the universe sending out a memo about something? The creators of M-Theory must have gotten it. Did I get it too? Furthermore, what if the Omniverse model is the small part that is missing from the top-down approach of M-Theory?

In the Omniverse model, we describe the theory from beginning to end on a time scale. However, true beginning occurs before the beginning of "real" time. The actual beginning is so far out in backwards time, also known as imaginary time, that it might be difficult to predict. It is like trying to predict the final fate of our universe in 150 billion years of real time in our future. However, the Omniverse model uses the laws of physics in order to show that history develops with real and imaginary time. Additionally, the quantum possibilities of all points in real time and imaginary time exist. This effectively cancels out time. It is appropriate to view the Omniverse as a model with all possibilities of time. The source, the point particle, the Inflationary Big Bang, and the expansion all exist as parts of one model. Each portion of the whole is entangled.

What M-Theory tells us is that these following conditions apply to its model because it applies to the top-down approach.

1) The laws of nature are apparent, depending on the history of the universe.
2) For different histories, the apparent laws are different.
3) The number of large dimensions, such as four-dimensional space-time, are not fixed by any set of the laws of physics.
4) There is a probability of amplitude for every large space-time dimension that ranges from 0-10.
5) Parallel universes exist with all possible internal spaces.[8]

Let us ask ourselves what the Omniverse model can become. If all information is contained in the point particle that becomes the Big Bang, the singularity can result in all possible variations of the Big Bang. Thus, one point particle results in an infinite number of parallel universes that each have their own apparent laws of physics. We only know the laws of physics in our universe because we can observe and quantify them. Therefore, Feynman's sum over histories applies to the Omniverse in the same way it does to M-Theory. The sum over histories results in infinite histories of the Big Bang and each history can have its own apparent laws of physics. Thus, we see that there might be some common ground if we connect the dots from the bottom of the Omniverse model to the top of M-Theory's approach.

We use eleven dimensions to describe the universe with M-Theory, but large dimensions are not fixed. Hawking stated that there should be few arbitrary variables in a system, but dimensions should be variable.[8] There is no reason in the first place to assume that there are only three or four dimensions. Three space dimensions give us x, y, and z. Einstein proposed space-time as a fourth dimension.

Then his work was presented in five dimensions. Further work in five large dimensions with six small dimensions is used to describe the apparent lack of gravity in our system compared to other forces. Our Omniverse model used a visual transformation from a three-dimensional system to a five-dimensional system. It is completely conceivable that this same approach could be used to describe an infinite amount of higher dimensions simply by repeating the pattern.

Let us talk about the passage of time while we are talking about time as a dimension. Time is measured by decay of matter. Thus, time does apply to our three space dimensions. This makes complete sense in Einsteinian four-dimensional space-time. However, there are different levels of decay. On the quantum scale, particles decay into forces or other particles. They might behave on a different time scale than ordinary matter. On the other side of the scale, there is the Omniverse model. Infinitely large, we produce a point particle in imaginary time. The decay of this particle can be represented by its destiny to become the Big Bang. Thus, we can also have three dimensions of "time" by looking at decay through multi-dimensional glasses.

There is an assumption that there is no limit to the amount of possible large dimensions in either model. We demonstrated that parallel universes are possible in both models. In addition, the probability of amplitude ranging from 0-10 is assigned to each large dimension. First, let us figure out what a probability of amplitude means. Our large dimensions are the most likely to have occurred in our universe. We would not be here otherwise. There is a probability of its existence for every dimension. This is rooted in statistical models.

Instead of looking at the probabilities of every dimension statistically, consider this. Imagine five large dimensions.

Quasicrystals occur in five dimensions with ordinary matter. The five-dimensional model offers some ways to understand light and gravity. The other six dimensions in M-Theory are small, curved dimensions in the formula. Curved dimensions? On paper, this would look like a swirl on the axis of a graph. There would be length inside the swirl, but it appears small. Other large dimensions are drawn out as having flat axes.

Ok, stop right there. Does this mean our dimensions are flat and others are curled? Why would this happen? Why would we assume that some are flat when others are curved? Why don't we say that all dimensions are curved, and the probability of curvature assigned to each large dimension would have a value ranging from 0-10? What we think is flat would be at the bottom of the scale. Additionally, the infinitely small and curved dimensions are on the other end. Modern science has proven that the Earth is not flat, so why do we assume that dimensions are flat? The flat-Earth belief might lead to a picture of the universe in which there is a point where you would literally fall of the edge. Ironically, according to our modern viewpoint there is a point where objects fall out of the universe forever. It is related to the accelerating expansion of the modern universe. This will be discussed in more detail later.

Now, let us look at the idea of curved dimensions. As we discussed earlier, the precise shape of these dimensions are determined mathematically by the value of physical quantities and the nature of the interactions between elementary particles. Stable orbits are possible with three large dimensions when following Newton's laws of motion. However, the orbits would be unstable with more than three large dimensions. In addition, gravitational attraction between bodies decreases with increasing number of dimensions.[8] These principles help us generalize three large dimensions that matter uses as guides for its building blocks, or directions with which to build upon.

The tightly curled dimensions are generally regarded as being unobservable because of their curvature. In other words, they might not affect Newton's laws at all. With the Omniverse model, we are also proposing that large dimensions are curved but to a lesser degree. Let us now visualize curved dimensions on a large scale that is observable. Instead of thinking of a graph with curved and spiraling axes, take a look at a globe. It is a sphere. In essence, it is just two dimensions consisting solely of x and y that are curved around the globe. Elevation is the third dimension, or the distance from the surface. Therefore, it is actually not hard at all to envision curved dimensions.

Recall how we transformed the surface of the globe onto a two-dimensional map. We saw that the gridlines were curved because of the surface distortion. And when we applied this to the expanding universe notion, it became the near-flat projection onto two larger dimensions that were part of an even bigger sphere. Thus, the larger dimensions are curved. This results in a slight curvature or distortion of the flattened bubble universe. However, this curvature is much less pronounced than is the curvature of our three dimensions. Therefore, they appear flatter. In summary, there is a probability of curvature assigned to each large dimension in the Omniverse model.

This gives me an idea of how to test and observe a portion of the Omniverse model. Omniverse and M-Theory are similar in the sense that they are incomplete. We might find some middle ground because the Omniverse is a bottom-up approach and M-Theory is a top-down approach. This would be a great achievement. However, it would be too early to jump to conclusions because there is so much more to both approaches.

When we compared the Omniverse model to superstrings, we found that there might be a potential conflict. The Omniverse contains the entire universe as a point particle, but superstrings had to abandon point particles. On the other hand, M-Theory becomes part of a bigger picture when it incorporates Superstring Theory. M-Theory used vibrating strings to describe physics as well as one-dimensional point particles, two-dimensional membranes, three-dimensional blobs, and other objects up to nine dimensions known as p-branes.[8,15]

The Omniverse model includes a point particle that is the pre-Big Bang singularity, containing all of the universe's information. The boundary between the two fields is similar to a two-dimensional membrane that has a degree of curvature. The transformed universe morphs from smooth and even in all directions into a flattened bubble of three or four dimensions. Thus, the universe is a blob or a p-brane, depending on the number of dimensions observed. It might be a 9-brane or higher if the source included all possible dimensions of the system. There seem to be many applications in which the Omniverse model can be tested by experts in the fields of physics. M-Theory has math with its top-down approach. The Omniverse model has a mechanism with the bottom-up approach. Only time will tell if they were meant to be together.

We will thus have successfully incorporated Quantum Mechanics, the General Theory of Relativity, Grand Unified Theory (GUT), and Supergravity if we can merge the simple geometry in the bottom-up Omniverse model to the top-down approach of M-Theory. We have examined the first three fields and have thus far qualitatively come out unscathed. By qualitatively, I mean pass or fail. There are no positive measurements such as a percentage scale involved in these examinations.

So what do we do with Supergravity, which introduced a graviton particle with a superpartner? It is also responsible for bringing Classical Relativity into the light of quantum physics. The problem is that we have not yet had the technology to detect these because the graviton requires such high energy in supercollider experiments. The search is nevertheless on, especially since scientists made the Higgs discovery with impeccable timing. The discovery was announced prior to the planned shutdown of the LHC for reworking and subsequent reopening in 2015.

The graviton is a force particle that should be consistent with the Omniverse because its existence is a consequence of mass in space-time. This means that it occurs after the Big Bang and thus would not conflict with the Omniverse model. The trick would be to experimentally identify and observe the anti-graviton. This could give us verification that the repulsive force exists. Repulsive force is the key to understanding the enigma of Dark Energy theories and also to the Omniverse model. The singularity would not have burst forth without this force, and the Big Bang would never have happened. We are currently on the lookout for repulsive forces in the next race to explain Dark Matter. Let's see next how this topic helps the Omniverse model, or vice versa.

Dark Energy versus Dark Matter

In this corner we have Dark Energy, the energy that must exist but has not yet been explained. In the other corner, we have Dark Matter that is a type of matter invisible to light that only appears to interact with ordinary matter through gravitational force. This match will be officiated by the Omniverse, the proposal that incorporates a model of the creation of the entire universe with external forces that affect the entire universe. Though this competition is an amusing notion, Dark Energy and Dark Matter do not really compete. In fact, they describe two completely different and mysterious phenomena. Perhaps what further studies of the Omniverse model need to question is if we can use this model to help solve the enigma of Dark Energy or Dark Matter.

Recall that nearly 68% of the energy of the universe as we know it comprises Dark Energy and that Dark Matter is approximately 27% while "normal" matter is less than 5%. Dark Matter is known as pressureless, non-relativistic matter that interacts weakly with matter particles of the Standard Model. What does this mean to us? We now know that the Higgs Mechanism involves weak interactions. Thus, a discovery of Dark Matter might be just around the corner. If it is subject to weak interactions, then it might interact with the Higgs Field to acquire mass just as ordinary matter does. However, there may be more mainstream approaches that help explain what some Dark Matter could be.

Planets and dead stars can be ejected from their orbits and be pushed out into the outermost reaches of a galaxy. Over time, this would amount to the adding up of dead weight within a galaxy with subsequent repetition of this process. But could there be enough momentum to be ejected from the galaxies? Galaxy clusters contain observable dark matter. When this was discovered, individual galaxies in a cluster were moving quickly enough to be able to escape the gravitational pull of the cluster. They should have been able to escape from the cluster if ordinary matter with visible mass was the only thing contributing to the cluster's gravitational pull. However, the cluster did not separate as expected. Thus, the existence of this "invisible" mass, or dark matter, was proposed by Zwicky in 1933.

Dark matter has been observed more recently as well. We previously discussed the collision of two clusters wherein most planets and stars pass through, but gasses are trapped more easily by the gravitational influence of the clusters. Therefore, the dark matter in the clusters can pass through unaffected while ordinary matter consisting mostly of gasses clump in the middle. Were there enough dead stars and ejected planets in this scenario, they would be able to pass each other without colliding because of the distances between the objects in these clusters.

The Higgs boson and mechanism's discovery was not the only monumental announcement of July 4, 2012. Another very significant observation pertaining to dark matter was also reported that same day. Dark matter was found in the filaments of our galaxy cluster. That 4th of July was really a fortuitous day for scientific advances. Are you feeling the new name for the "Independence Age" of science? Filaments are like fingers in the outermost parts of the clusters. They are similar to the outermost fingers of the galaxies where dead material builds up. This observed filament of dark matter stretched between two different clusters. It looks like a huge string of dark matter because of its distance from us, but what it is made up of remains unknown.

There would have to be a mechanism that keeps generating matter or antimatter and recycling for these recent observations to be explained by ejected material. This would require the mechanism to build more and more matter over billions of years, which is observed in the life cycles of galactic objects. There are regions of galaxies where matter is still actively being produced. Dark matter could build up over time as planets and stars live and die through their cycles. Other recent observational data has shown that dark matter builds up along the outer edges of galaxies.

This is an ongoing process. Over time, ejected planets and dead stars are spun off to the outermost parts of galaxies and then toward the filaments of galaxy clusters. While it is feasible to envision dark matter as dead planets and stars, the quantity that would be enough to account for all of the known dark matter is unknown. In addition, dark matter outnumbers ordinary matter more than six times to one. Ejected matter may only account for a portion of all dark matter.

If we have that much more dark matter than ordinary matter, are there any other alternatives to explain it? What else would give us an excess of gravity? If we have theorized gravitational leakage into a fifth dimension where gravity is stronger, could we have pieces of fifth-dimensional matter?

It sounds far-fetched, but what if the bubbles of the universe with our laws of physics are not filled in completely? There might be a way that higher-dimensional bubbles exist with different apparent laws of nature. Such bubbles could have strong regional gravity, thus warping space-time. They would be like "spots" throughout the universe wherein gravitational leakage to a higher dimension occurs. This makes me wonder what gravitational leakage would entail. Is it an exchange of information with a repulsive antigravity force throughout the universe? If we have a continued influx of repulsive force from the Omniverse, can that repulsive force be split into gravitons and anti-gravitons? If so, is it conceivable that one would provide extra gravity while the other provides repulsion?

However, gravity and expansion are not equal from what we can observe in the universe. The repulsive forces outnumber the gravitational forces of dark matter almost three to one. This is truly the biggest enigma of physics today. Almost 70% of the universe is dark energy. We really don't know what else to call it. It seems somewhat odd to call it "dark" because this simply means that it is unknown.

While dark energy has been theorized and its effects recognized, it has not been observed. We know it affects our universe because dark energy provides the energy that causes repulsion within the universe. Such energy pushes galaxies and galaxy clusters away from each other. There are still regions of attraction in the universe, but it is mostly spreading. Moreover, that spreading accelerates with greater distances from the observer.

This expansion is an observable occurrence. Dark energy is a negative pressure throughout the universe. We know that expansion is happening. Dark energy is our only hope of explaining why this happens. However, the mathematical models get very complex in order to explain the infinite nature of the acceleration. Mathematical models do not like infinities.

As we discussed, most models use Einstein's cosmological constant. The cosmological constant is basically vacuum energy density. This means that there is a value assigned to space that represents the expansion. However, the cosmological constant is typically large and consequently problematic.

Using the modified gravity approach, the late-time acceleration of the universe can be realized as a result of gravitational leakage from a three-dimensional surface into a fifth extra dimension.[9] Another recent model thus incorporates five-dimensional gravitational leakage. However, it is used in this instance in order to explain the surplus of negative pressure or repulsion in the universe. It should be noted that the theories involving gravitational leakage are not unique to the Omniverse theory. In this model higher dimensions are used to help visualize the Omniverse to clarify the various processes. There is very likely an underlying cycle involving a constant influx of repulsive force.

This possibility is where the Omniverse model can gain strength. It involves the transmutation of repulsive force from the primary field in at least five dimensions. This force is translated into expansion beneath the surface of the primary field's boundary with the secondary field. The Omniverse model provides a source for energy within a framework of extra dimensions. Moreover, this energy of repulsive forces leaking into the three-dimensional universe we observe might then split into gravitons and anti-gravitons in order to explain dark matter and dark energy respectively. Somehow, it seems, the universe must know how much energy it needs of each form in order to maintain the delicate balance of its system.

In summary, the Omniverse model may be helpful in determining or providing adjustments to work already in progress for the source and cause of dark energy. Further work in this field needs to be performed while the Omniverse model needs to be tested and validated.

The Holographic Omniverse

I keep thinking about what I said earlier about the point particle containing all of the information in the universe. The point particle becomes the Big Bang when it leaves the primary field and enters a secondary field. Then the universe is literally projected through rapid inflation into the fabric of space-time. This one point particle is very similar to a hologram. It contains all of the universe's information that is projected as it is activated in the presence of energy. In the case of a hologram, light manipulates an image on a two-dimensional surface in order to project a three-dimensional image. In the case of the holographic universe, primordial energy from outside the known universe activates a hologram into a projection of at least eleven dimensions.

The universe is moving from a higher state of energy to a lower one as it enters inflation. This process involves breaking symmetry and letting go of energy. Perhaps this energy stimulates a holographic projection from the point particle. However, the projection might change over time if the point particle is non-static. For example, we might see an increase in the expansion of the universe if it was moving away from the stronger primary field while more of it reacts to the weaker secondary field. On the other hand we might see the universe clumping if it was moving back into the primary field. It seems the field may have a mix of attraction and repulsion, but we have observed our universe to be spreading over time. Therefore, it is less likely that we would see a particle going back into the primary field in the Omniverse model because we have observed the universe in an accelerating state of expansion. It appears to be an ongoing reaction of symmetry breaking and energy levels dropping while light, matter, and mass form and continually expand.

And if the universe is indeed a holographic projection of the point particle, it would also explain another bizarre subject known as spooky-action-at-distance. We know that quantum entanglement happens. It has been observed in experiments that have been repeated successfully. We have started to control this process and gain some basic understanding of it. But do we know why it happens? Entanglement happens because every fundamental force, particle, and wave in our universe is essentially from this point. The perceived separation is measured in terms of distance and time, but in a system with all quantum possibilities of time coexisting, entanglement is a consequence.

Just as time cancels itself out with quantum possibilities involving time and imaginary time, we might get the same effect with distance. If distance cancels itself out, then the particles that are several billion light years away are still part of the original point particle at zero distance. These distant particles are still part of the point particle before inflation. Every atom inside of us and every subatomic particle inside of those as well as every force and anti-particle are thus linked back to a single point in space and time. This sounds consistent with a holographic theory. If everything is entangled, then we are literally one with our universe.

8

PUT IT TO THE TEST

"Since life is an ever-evolving process, one should follow in this process and discover how to actualize and expand oneself."

—Bruce Lee

We have thus far put the Omniverse model to the test when comparing it to the hundreds of years of scientific advances and countless observations. But we ultimately need to find ways of testing, predicting, and observing features of the Omniverse in order to validate the model. In the last chapter, it seemed to pass qualitatively with all of the major theories we have covered. The next step would be to verify the model with mathematics.

I am asking the scientific community to collaborate in this task. In the spirit of getting instant answers, I also want to point out that while writing this book, an independent team of Canadian physicists published a paper in 2013 (available at http://arxiv.org/pdf/1309.1487v1.pdf)[19] detailing a system very similar to what I have described with the Omniverse model. As previously noted, synchronicities sometimes occur independently by separate parties.

This section will present some of the ways that we might predict and observe phenomena that are related to the Omniverse model. We will discuss them in terms of how they do or do not support the proposal.

Repeating Patterns

One of the first things I noticed about the universe was that there seemed to be shapes that repeat themselves similar to fractals. Shapes repeat from smaller structures to larger structures. Following this logic, why would this trend stop when we view our universe as a whole? This is how I had the idea that the universe was just part of a larger cycle called the Omniverse.

The repeating patterns will help us visualize and understand the possibilities of infinity. Let's start from the smallest of the small. Every particle at the quantum level is paired with a force. This was a concept taken from Supersymmetry. A Higgs boson is paired with the Higgs Field via the weak force. Quarks are paired with force particles via the strong force to form subatomic particles.

At the atomic level, the three subatomic particles form a nucleus and an electron field. It should be noted that when we speak about an electron as a field, it is important to understand that the traditional approach with an electron orbiting a nucleus is no longer considered correct. An electron exists as a field or several fields around the nucleus. These fields interact with other atoms and transmit energies. We see orbits that occur as a function of gravity at the scale larger than atoms. Moons orbit planets and planets orbit stars. Solar systems orbit supermassive black holes in galaxies.

Supermassive black holes were a recent 20th century discovery, with several indirect observations made with the Spitzer Space Telescope in the 21st century. When it was postulated that our galaxy and others had supermassive black holes, I realized this pattern must exist on a higher level. In the Omniverse model, I found this comparable to what would be considered a supermassive white hole. This white hole's power would be roughly equivalent to all of the supermassive black holes in the universe combined. As you can see, there are similar attributes on all of the scales. The solar systems, planets, moons, atoms, subatomic particles, quarks, et cetera all have similar yet distinct patterns. History repeats itself as does the physical world.

Along with each repetition from quantum to supermacro scales, there is also this key observation. Each has its own individual process while generally mimicking the levels above and below. The Omniverse has repulsive and high pressure forces. A supermassive black hole has attractive forces so strong that even light cannot escape it. The planetary orbits have a fatal consequence of falling into the sun in their system given enough time. Electrons have multiple fields or states. Though not all properties are directly transferrable, there are similarities between all scenarios. Our Omniverse model resembles this pattern with the universe as a field surrounding the source. Moreover, the Omniverse could have multiple states similar to electron orbitals that result in additional universes with different laws of physics.

One comparison is that of the event horizon, or the point of no return. An atom exchanges its outer electron or electrons. A planet eventually falls into its sun. A supermassive black hole sucks in matter at will. An Omniverse pushes away particles that create universes. The event horizon in the Omniverse is the boundary of the primary and secondary field wherein our universe is born and spread across. What ensues is a multidimensional exchange of energies that create the hologram and fuel the processes within the universe. So the first step of observing phenomena would be to demonstrate that higher dimensions are real. But how do we prove that multiple dimensions are even real? As it turns out, we have a recent discovery in 2010 that may do just that.

Proof of Multiple Dimensions

It would be difficult to prove the existence of higher dimensions directly related to dimensional leakage or interchange of gravity and other such forces. However, we can look at a more general view of multiple dimensions in real-life objects that you can touch and feel.

One might ask if we can see objects in more than three dimensions. Well, yes, we can. But this story has another twist.

Back in the early 1990s, I studied the phenomenon known as quasicrystals. This was shortly after graduating with a degree in geology, so the mathematical crystallography concepts were still relatively fresh in my mind. I learned that metallurgists had been working with alloys using two or three different types of atoms, and they produced a freak-of-nature phenomenon that became known as quasicrystals. But don't confuse these with actual crystals. Quasicrystals are different in how they form and how they look.

Quasicrystals were first proposed in the 1980s by Israeli scientist Daniel Schechtman. Unfortunately, he was not treated well by mainstream scientists for his discovery. Nevertheless, his work was recognized when he received a Nobel Prize in 2011. Thus, quasicrystals are now accepted by the scientific community. Why are they so unique and unbelievable? Quasicrystals have five-sided symmetry. This means that they can be rotated along an axis five times and the symmetry is the same. A pentagon, or five-sided polygon, is a good example of five-way symmetry. However, no true crystals can have five-sided symmetry. It was a mathematical impossibility in terms of crystal lattices. A crystal lattice is assembled in three dimensions and has a basic repeating pattern. However, the way metal alloys bond is different from crystal lattices. The quasicrystals were basically metal atoms that were stacked atop each other. This is typical of metals and their alloys. But the manner in which they were stacked resulted in pseudo-crystals with five sides.

Metallurgists had produced five-sided quasicrystals with their proprietary alloys. Crystallographers use matrices to calculate the symmetries of the quasicrystals being made in laboratories. The number of dimensions is determined by how many numbers are put in the matrix. More dimensions in the matrix were defined in order to depict the structure of quasicrystals. The added dimensions are described as mathematical dimensions. There may not be a direct correlation to mathematical and physical dimensions, however. The take-away is that there are ways to describe more than three dimensions. Typically six or more were used to mathematically describe quasicrystals.

Such quasicrystals were never found in nature. They were custom fabricated under precise conditions. Thus, quasicrystals had only been produced in laboratories. Scientists figured out exactly how much of each metal to use in an alloy and exactly what conditions were needed for the metal atoms to stack in particular ways. But in 2010 a rare find in Russia yielded a meteorite with naturally occurring quasicrystals. While the meteorite's origin has been debated, it appears to be authentic and verifies that these rare forms do exist in nature. Therefore, this was supporting evidence that there can be more than three dimensions in nature.

Ripples in the Outer Dimensions

Cosmic microwave background radiation studies have helped us define the view of our universe shortly after the Big Bang. Our picture of nearly uniform cosmic microwave background, or CMB, was taken by three different satellite observatories. The first was COBE in 1992 and then WMAP in 2001 followed by the European Space Agency's Planck space telescope in 2013. But they did not send up three space observatories to capture the same imagery. Each successive generation was on a mission to scan the CMB in greater detail. WMAP's data acquisition took place over a period from 2001 to 2010. Planck was launched in 2009, and its initial data had only been collected over a period of 15.5 months. Planck's findings, announced in March 2013, gave more accurate representations of the age and makeup of the universe. Furthermore, additional data is expected from the Planck mission.

The successively greater detail provided by the WMAP and Planck missions has given scientists a better establishment of the model used to describe the history and structure of the universe. WMAP estimated the age of the universe to within one percent and found it to be 13.75 billion years old. Its components were 4.6% normal matter and 22.7% dark matter, leaving the remaining 72% as dark energy. These estimates were revised with data from Planck in 2013. The age of the universe is now 13.82 billion years with normal matter making up 4.9%, dark matter 26.8%, and dark energy 68.3% of the universe. The CMB observed also provided proof of early inflation in the Big Bang. The three missions have shown us that the residual heat of the Big Bang appears nearly uniform over the entire sky, as was shown in Figure 2.

There are also more details emerging from the shape of the background, mainly in the form of cosmic ripples. They found that the angular size of the ripples in the CMB is connected to the composition of the universe. The observations of WMAP show that the ripples were approximately one degree across, or about twice the size of Earth's moon. However, there were some arguments based upon telescopic smoothing regarding the size of the ripples. The details are still under debate. Regardless of the exact size and nature of cosmic ripples, we should focus on the fact that ripples have been observed. Rather than discuss measurement techniques or statistical analyses, we will discuss the significance of the ripples and how this affects our physical model of the universe.

This discovery is something that physicists had been talking about for a long time with great anticipation. So what are cosmic ripples? They are the leftover energy from the very beginning of the universe. The detected cosmic microwave background is about 380,000 years from the beginning of post-inflation time. It is still a blink of an eye compared to the 13.82 billion year age of the universe. The early light would transform itself to lower wavelengths over time and distance, thus becoming cosmic background radiation over time. This observation gives us a great picture of the early universe, but we want to look even earlier in its formation. The ripples are from the first trillionth of a second of the universe.

The ripples give us a much closer look toward the point when time began and inflation dominated the very early universe. The Omniverse model shows us why we might see ripples. The point particle is hurled away from the source and primary high-energy field and then reaches the secondary field that behaves as if it were a liquid. As the point particle "splashes" into the secondary lower energy field, it creates ripples along the field's boundary. Think of symmetry breaking and creating shock waves similar to ripples on the surface of a smooth pond of water. In the inflationary model, these ripples might correlate to the initial rapid expansion of space before light and matter were born. The ripples create the zone of influence wherein space expands in the beginning of the universe.

The ripples have applications in support of the Omniverse proposal. In addition, much of the earlier work that I used to contribute to this model will also benefit from the observations of cosmic ripples. Maxwell's theory of light, electromagnetic force, weak-force bosons, and the strong force were found to be consistent in the fifth dimension when Einstein's equations were applied in five dimensions. This was like a unification of forces, or a picture of the underlying force. Moreover, it was predicted that light would be observable via ripples in the fifth dimension that correspond to visible light waves in four-dimensional space-time. Can this form of ripples be what has been observed? We have ripples forming in the early Inflationary Big Bang followed by the formation of photons in the early universe. These ripples may tell us much more about our universe than what is just on the surface. The universe literally forms under the surface where these ripples are observed.

Given enough time and data to study this further, ripples in the beginning of the universe can help scientists unify forces with a mechanism that has measurable consequences in the real world. These studies will lead to major successes in physics if such mechanisms can be observed and quantified. I believe the Omniverse model will also provide a geometric principle that may allow scientists to visualize multi-dimensional phenomena. Such observations could help explain the universe in terms of a bigger picture, describing where the universe came from. For now, ripples help us observe the effects of the Omniverse's mechanism as well as other five-dimensional theories involving forces.

Accelerated Expansion of the Current Universe

The phenomenon known as dark energy has been theorized to be pressureless repulsive forces that cause continuing expansion of the universe and accelerate expansion.[17] We will use the Omniverse model as a geometric principle that may provide guidance in the studies of dark energy using curved dimensional lensing. I am proposing this technique along with the Omniverse model. I believe this may have a very good chance to show observable and measurable consequences of the higher-dimensional system of the Omniverse model. We will discuss this topic in the next section and suggest directions for conducting a basic experiment in order to test this mechanism.

We may find that we are viewing the entire universe through a lens. This lens distorts the image in the outermost corners similar to our projection of the globe onto two dimensions. Recall that this projection showed curvature of the gridlines. We know that gravitational lensing affects light in such a way that we can measure gravitational effects with great accuracy. Lensing is a known technique and it has been used for many years. In 2012, this technique was used to illustrate how dark matter forms filaments between two galaxy clusters. But this is all lensing within our universe.

What the Omniverse model suggests is that we would see another level of lensing that affects the entire universe by using a similar mechanism of known lensing effects inside the universe. That means the observation may be testable and measurable. With enough quantified data, it could be shown to have statistical accuracy. This is the ultimate goal of science. The Omniverse model has a long way to go, but we could move forward with the model and find other ways to test it and observe its effects in space-time if we devise experiments that quantify some of its features. First we should develop a model and find ways to test it. We then predict how it affects the universe and look to see if data bolsters the observations.

So how do we make the Omniverse model explain that the universe is being viewed through a curved lens? The answer is actually quite simple. Let's pick up our globe again. We transformed its three dimensions into two dimensions by viewing it as a nearly flattened ellipsis. We placed the flattened object onto the surface of a bigger spherical feature. This resulted in a slight warping of our three-dimensional projection onto the two-dimensional surface. Thus, our three dimensions were shown to be curved along the surface. We had a nearly flattened bubble that was stretched out along the surface of a larger sphere.

Consider the physical characteristics of our curved bubble. If it is curved, the degree of curvature is then related to the apparent size of the higher-dimensional shape. This can be measured in space. I will show you how, but let us first see why this happens. Figure 9 shows us a slice of the nearly flattened bubble curved across a surface. The arrows indicate the directions of expansion.

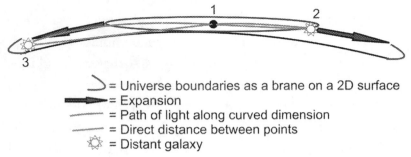

= Universe boundaries as a brane on a 2D surface
= Expansion
= Path of light along curved dimension
= Direct distance between points
= Distant galaxy

Figure 9 Curvature of Four-Dimensional Space-Time: This shows a cross sectional view of the curvature of a spherical higher-dimensional object with four-dimensional space-time projected onto its two-dimensional surface.

Expansion occurs in all directions in our universe. But when projected to two dimensions, expansion occurs along that surface. This is similar to going into a black hole with strings. Information gets spread out along the event horizon until such information is evenly spread across the entire object. Thus, information is not lost in this system.

We are seeing this occur as our bubble is continually expanding along the surface of the higher-dimensional object. The higher-dimensional object acts as if it were a supergiant white hole. Our universe's information is spread along the surface of the higher dimensional event horizon. Note that this description of expansion does not involve any loss of information. Recall our discussion of the black hole event horizon paradox wherein the loss of information was solved by realizing that information entering a black hole is spread across its event horizon, thus preventing loss. On the other hand, would we experience a loss of information if the universe's expansion was accelerating everything into nothingness?

We are not experiencing a loss of information with the Omniverse model because it is being evenly spread along the event horizon of a white hole. This explains our expansion that appears to be accelerating to us in our universe. Such phenomena also provide an observable degree of curvature of our universe. This observation comes to us in a way that we may have already observed but has the capability to change the way we interpret the observed data. The acceleration of the universe's expansion that we observe and quantify today is this lensing effect at work. It is caused by the curvature of the system that we are projected from, as illustrated in Figure 9. An interesting point of comparison is the Randall-Sundrum model of five-dimensional gravity, which also uses a curved or warped surface.

How does the curvature make us observe accelerated expansion in the outermost reaches of the universe? When we add curvature to the equation, we see that light (shown as curved lines) follow a longer path between us and the observed object than does the line-of-sight distance (straight lines) because light follows a curved path in such a case. The curved path, or apparent distance, translates into a straight line within our three or four dimensional space. On the other hand, the line-of-sight distance is represented as the straight line in higher dimensional space. Therefore, light's apparent distance is greater than the direct distance. In addition, this effect's amplitude is increased based upon the observed object's distance to the observer. Thus, the farther an object travels from the observer, the faster it appears to be moving away. Objects eventually accelerate out of view as they encounter the event horizon at the edge of our observable universe.

Look at point 1 in Figure 9. This represents the center of our observable universe. This point in four-dimensional space-time would be the middle of our uniform, spherical universe. We pick two objects of known distance from this point. Points 2 and 3 represent galaxies far away from the observer, but point 2 is closer to us than is point 3. As you can see in both cases, when the observed distance is determined by the curved pathway, it is longer than the actual distance shown as a straight line. For point 3, the apparent distance from the object along a curved surface is greater. This shows how the lensing effect amplifies the apparent distance of objects that are farther away from the observer.

This effect would distort our view of the universe in our four-dimensional space-time. If object 2 is closer to us but moving away and object 3 is farther away and still moving away, the curved pathway of the light makes it appear that object 3 is moving away faster because it seems to be a greater distance than it actually is. Just as we have observed, we would see objects that are farther away as accelerating because expansion pulls them farther away from us when we apply this principle to the known universe.

What does this mean for physics today? For starters, this technique can be used to study the pressureless force of dark energy that is thought to cause expansion. If you have to calculate expansion as accelerating, it becomes infinity. This can be problematic because mathematics can't handle infinities. On the other hand, the actual distance is shorter if you understand that light is following a curved higher dimensional surface. A model of dark energy with linear distances would be much simpler than a model with an accelerating variable. Therefore, the energy of the entire system in the Omniverse model could provide a constant influx of energy that leads to expansion. This would be related to distance increasing in a linear, non-accelerating fashion if the influx is constant. However, it would appear to an observer in a bubble as if the farthest objects were accelerating. Thus, one should question a universe wherein objects literally accelerate beyond the observable edge.

So far, we have used real-world observed and quantified phenomena to back up the approach of proposing the Omniverse model. Whether ripples are real or not is currently under debate within the scientific communities. We have observed and measured ripples and await confirmation that the data is indeed valid. Expansion is also real, observable, and measurable. And these are explained and graphically depicted by projecting four-dimensional space-time onto a higher-dimensional surface. It is my hope that such transformations can be mathematically verified by using advanced theoretical techniques such as M-Theory. Only time will tell. That and experiments.

Experiments are the cornerstone of modern science. Each discussion of the Omniverse model provides a recommendation for further studies to experimentally verify the model. As we will see in the next section, I have a simple experiment that can be used to demonstrate the lensing effect from the curvature of the two-dimensional projection of space-time.

Lensing Experiment

When I was in college physics, we had to watch a movie in grainy black and white from the 1950s on the points of view of different systems in motion. With a narrator using that obviously 1950s voice, he described how our perception can change the way we understand systems. It actually applies to modern science today. They filmed actors sitting in chairs on a circular stage and the background was moving around them. But was the background moving, or were they moving? This is basically the same principle we are trying to show with the perception of accelerating expansion in our universe. Is it really accelerating, or does it only appear to be?

I propose an experiment by which we can test the lensing effect due to the curvature of higher dimensions. This can give us a glimpse into whether acceleration can be a function of curvature of a system. This experiment requires a simple set-up. It would involve a camera with interchangeable lenses and some uniformly round objects such as hula-hoops. Sounds like fun, doesn't it?

First, mount the camera in a fixed position with a tripod. Now, this may be a little tricky, but we need to be able to move a hula-hoop toward the camera in a succession of fixed positions. The hula-hoop also will be moved toward the camera until it goes out of view of the camera's lens. The pictures should be at uniform intervals.

From the viewpoint through the camera's lens, the hula-hoop would appear to be moving outward from the center. Therefore, the hula-hoop appears smaller in the frame when it is farther away from the camera. Keep taking pictures as it moves closer and gets bigger in the camera's viewfinder. Next, we would measure the circles from the center of each picture. Each picture should show bigger circles as the hula-hoop gets closer to the camera until out of view. We should see an apparent accelerating of the diameter of the circles in the photographs as the hula-hoop moves out of view. Moreover, this acceleration should be proportional to the curvature of the camera lens.

Now let's go to the next step. We are going to repeat the first step, but this time we will use a lens such as a fish-eye or wide-angle lens that has greater curvature. The distance intervals of the hula-hoop must be exactly the same. However, we should see an apparent acceleration of the circles that is greater than was seen with the first lens because of the increased distortion of a lens with greater curvature. With greater curvature, the apparent acceleration will be more pronounced.

Each of these two steps should be repeated enough times in order to have a large enough data set that would achieve statistical significance. This experiment should be conducted in controlled conditions and be able to acquire a data set of observable and measurable distances from the center of each photograph. In the end, the experiment should show that distortion due to curvature will exaggerate distances from the center as the circles approach the edge of the field of view.

That being said, the curvature causing the apparent acceleration can be translated to the curvature of the higher dimensions that was explained in the previous section. We would see when applying this principle that expansion is linear, much like the constant speed of hula-hoops approaching the camera. However, the lensing effect causes it to look like distant objects are accelerating away from us. This can be explained by the curved path that the light takes in order to get from the object to the observer. This curved path is directly proportional to the curvature of the system.

I would encourage those reading to try this experiment on your own and see what kind of results you get. Or, you could come up with other experiments I haven't thought of. It's not required, though. I don't want to give people homework. But I do want to present at least one way the Omniverse model can be tested. From the concept of curved space-time, this approach seems entirely feasible. And this approach is incorporated within the Omniverse model.

To summarize, we should be able to detect a signature of perceived expansion based on the curvature of the lens. When applied to the Omniverse model, the repulsive forces cause this lensing effect in the universe as a whole. Recall Einstein's work uncovering space-time warping that is caused by gravity. This caused the two-dimensional surface of space-time to warp downwards. When the repulsive forces are applied to the same model, we see a regional upward warping of space-time. This warping is why we observe expansion within our universe.

THE TAKE-AWAY

"You can see love everywhere in this creation
if only you have the eyes to see it."
—*Sri Sri Ravi Shankar*

If someone comes up to you and asks what is in space, how would you answer now that you have experienced the Omniverse? After reading this book, I hope your answer is everything. Space is not empty and has never been. It is teeming with energies. These energies are observed in the forms of fields, forces, and projections of matter. All of space contains the basic building blocks for creating universes. The building blocks of a universe begin to assemble after a point particle interacted with a field that sufficiently energized the system. It is a wind-up toy! The one doing the winding is the Omniverse. Therefore, the take-away of this knowledge is that we and the universe are a part of something bigger.

A New Beginning

In the Omniverse model proposed in this book, we discussed how a singularity, also known as point particle, interacts with two fields in order to create the universe via the Inflationary Big Bang. The singularity is just a point particle when it is in the right conditions. While surrounded by high energies and limitless dimensions, it has no dimensions yet with no time and no distance in its early state. It exists only as a Planck length across, which is smaller than anything measurable by human standards. The point particle simply cannot remain stable in its form under different conditions. After all, this particle is full of all of the energy contained in the universe. However, it does experience different conditions as it goes from the primary higher energy field to the secondary lower energy field and experiences a breaking of symmetry. The result of its energy is the creation of the Big Bang.

Modern science already has a model for the Big Bang Theory and its inflationary modifications, so why would we change that? We do not because the Omniverse model changes nothing about the Inflationary Big Bang. Instead, it attempts to fill in the gaps regarding events before and after the Big Bang. It answers the question of how the singularity got there before it became the Big Bang. The Omniverse provides a mechanism that leads to the conditions in which the Inflationary Big Bang can exist.

Until now, humanity has not been able to explain what happened before the Big Bang because time starts from that moment, and it has been assumed that events before the Big Bang would have no consequences afterward. Now everything is changing and assumptions are overturned with this proposal. The Omniverse model adds the before and after picture to what is currently known about the universe's creation.

Few scientists have made theories about what creates the Big Bang while others have abandoned the approach with their reasoning or beliefs. According to Steven Hawking, one of the greatest minds in the history of science, we could not use events before the Big Bang to determine what would happen afterward because predictability would break down at time-zero of the Big Bang. Therefore, events that may or may not have occurred before the Big Bang would have no consequence. Thus, they cannot inform a scientific model of the universe.[1] While Hawking is not one I would want to disagree with, I think Hawking's approach can be misleading. Such assertions did not deter Guth who modified the theory in order to show how inflation occurred in the "bang" of the Big Bang. Rather than allow Hawking's assertion to deter me, I argued that events before the Big Bang do affect our reality and proposed events that occurred before inflation.

To reason away the beginning does not answer the questions regarding the origin of the universe. Where did it come from? How did it get there? How was the singularity able to exist before the Big Bang started if the singularity was not stable? I argue that the beginning does matter and that such inquiries may help further inform current universe theories. Furthermore, I believe that the Omniverse model allows us to view the mechanism of the universe's origin while helping to answer questions regarding expansion of the universe. I believe that this will ultimately become a theory that describes the universe as a whole by placing it within a larger framework. Perhaps we can understand the Omniverse model as a bigger picture. This proposal describes the universe as a whole with only a few elements and makes predictions regarding the types of observations that will support it.

I used guidelines from Hawking's works to create new theories in order to present this model of the Omniverse. I incorporated Feynman's sum over histories regarding how a particle follows every possible path in space-time. Histories were presented in real time and in imaginary time, or a negative value that is indistinguishable from directions in space. We saw that this effectively cancels space-time, meaning that there is a universe with all possibilities of time or distance. Einstein's curved space-time caused by gravity was also used in the new model, and an additional concept of large-scale dimensional curving was introduced. Finally, we attempted to make predictions based on the quantum possibilities and observations of the currently known universe.

Hawking was one of the first resources that I researched in order to learn about the universe. There are many other contributors to the works that I researched. Michio Kaku was the one who originally sparked my idea. I saw him on television back in the 1990s. He was saying that someday someone would find a simple equation that was only about an inch long that described everything in the universe as we know it. That idea stuck in my head. Is it possible to create a simple equation that describes everything?

I took a slightly different approach and instead of creating an equation, my mind envisioned a simple geometric mechanism that grew to become the Omniverse model. The mechanism's basic geometric principle underlying the mechanism fits Kaku's description, only with minimal math. I was able to see a basic "flow" equation of the total energies in the universe. I believe the "missing" source of dark energy in our universe can be explained with the Omniverse model. Energy in the form of repulsion and pressure should balance out the universe's energies from forces, matter, dark matter, and gravity. We have to look outside of our universe and view this system of forces as a whole in order to find these energies.

The Omniverse proposal uses the known laws of physics in order to show how history develops with time and imaginary time. We started with simple geometry and then described the action. The action was then used to make predictions about the theory. We presented the concept of how the mechanism works in the Omniverse model. We put it to the test by presenting ways its features might be observable. Let us recap.

- We showed how patterns repeat themselves in a fractal manner. We found that each subsequent generation of patterns that were observed in the structures of atoms, solar systems, galaxies, clusters, and the Omniverse were unique. However, each repeated its basic properties on different scales.

- We saw how multiple dimensions are easy to visualize with stacking and realized that higher dimensions may help us resolve our biggest questions about the universe.
- We used the model to represent the multi-dimensional Omniverse as an expanding bubble on a curved surface in the present time. By viewing our dimensions flattening across a larger curved surface, we found that this explained why the universe looks like its expansion accelerates in the outer reaches of space beyond the point of no return.
- Finally, we proposed a simple experiment to test the phenomenon of expanding across large curved hidden dimensions.

We put the Omniverse model through additional tests by qualitatively comparing it to historic and modern scientific knowledge of the universe. The model was screened for inconsistencies or incompatibilities with Newton's laws of physics, classical theory, and quantum physics, including the latter's latest and greatest branch, M-Theory. We found general agreement with all concepts, and there is no conflict with the Omniverse model where current theories describe the inflationary Big Bang model. This is because the Omniverse model incorporates the Big Bang as part of the process. This model attempts to fill in gaps regarding what happens before and after the Big Bang. We may have also found that what happens afterward might be different from previous beliefs.

The Omniverse proposal is a model that uses the bottom-up approach that describes the theory from the beginning. I read during my research that M-Theory is a top-down approach to a physical theory and therefore has no underlying geometric principle. While it is too early to make any definitive conclusions, there does appear to be a possible middle ground between the two. Could this be the geometric principle we are looking for that will make the theories complete? I stated in the beginning of this book that all of the different theories seemed to fit as if they were pieces of a puzzle or continents on our globe. We are now seeing that all of the pieces can fit together.

Scientists made the initial observation that the continents seemed to fit together even though they were separated by oceans when Plate Tectonics was introduced. Scientists found fossils on one continent that matched the age of similar fossils on other continents. We started seeing evidence of a possible match. As technology increased, we were finally able to conclude that the continents did originally fit together and that there was a mechanism called continental drift. Plate tectonics was driven by an underlying energy in the form of magma beneath the Earth's crust. Furthermore, the phenomenon was observable in fault lines and volcanic eruptions around the globe.

The Omniverse model is the initial observation wherein the theories of the universe fit together like a puzzle. It has an underlying energy responsible for the process of creating the Big Bang. We will enter the next phase of discovery as we observe, measure, and accumulate data as time and technology allow. So now that this model has been presented, the next step is to put it out to the scientific communities of the world. The Omniverse model could be the beginning of something new, something bigger than ever before reasoned. This concept should ultimately make us question everything we know about our universe, including how we perceive it.

Consciousness and the Omniverse

We took a look inside the human psyche and the concept of mind before exploring the scientific aspects of the Omniverse model. We were able to visualize the mind as the fields of thought that we generate and interact with on both the conscious and subconscious levels. One can picture the mind outside one's body, growing as you become aware of your surroundings with your eyes closed while meditating. With this technique, you can literally feel your surroundings. Allow the concept of the mind to expand as you perceive more around you. There is no limit as to how far you can go.

I would highly recommend taking a meditation course or following guided meditations if you are interested. Meditation allows the mind to rest in a state of lower energy, like the universe, and provides several health benefits. It can also lower the frequency of brainwaves, thus making it possible to experience one's subconscious. It may also allow one to understand these concepts better in your own way by observing the underlying energy yourself. It is my hope that this practice will give everyone the perspective that we are all a part of something bigger.

Reflect back on yourself through this process now that you know something about the Omniverse proposal. How has this affected you? How do you feel now? Do you think that you are part of a higher presence, or part of something bigger than the universe? Can you actually become one with the universe? Can you visualize higher dimensions wherein basic information exchanges yield our known laws of physics and all of the forces and matter contained in our universe? Are you aware of an underlying energy that drives the mechanism and creates all forces, fields, and matter in our universe? The Omniverse might show us the answers to all of these questions. We of the universe ask, and the Omniverse answers. But how you feel regarding the concept is entirely up to you. It is my hope that it will leave a lasting impression of unity with one's surroundings and a feeling of expansion of one's consciousness.

Sri Sri Ravi Shankar had once said to me that the universe was made up of pure love. I have gained an understanding of what he meant after studying the universe. Our perception of the underlying energy feels like love, also known as the "law of attraction." It is responsible for every possibility of energy creating every single particle that is coming together in order to form matter that we use when defining our reality.

By reading this book, I hope the reader will experience this feeling by being in such a state of mind wherein you are visualizing the Omniverse concepts. I want everyone to walk away from this book with a better understanding and a better feeling regarding themselves and their surroundings. Additionally, I give permission to use any of the work presented herein for further studies regarding the subjects discussed. I am putting it out to the world to accept our newly discovered destiny within an Omniverse that is responsible for creating our universe.

Will we abandon the notion of a universe wherein one can literally fall off the edge at some distant point? We did exactly that when we discovered that the Earth was round. I sincerely hope that we can advance our collective knowledge without bias from beliefs of religion or lack thereof or attachment to current beliefs that prevent acceptance of change. We will inevitably change how we view our creation. We will overcome our limitations of understanding by employing a model that incorporates a bigger picture.

I ask the readers to help spread the word about the Omniverse. If the scientific community can find ways to test this model by using mathematical concepts, it is my wish that as many people as possible work together in order to solve the universe's biggest questions. Please note that I do not intend for any of this material to be used in any argument of religion versus science. We are all trying to describe the same thing and find different ways to do it. After all, I did it with a baseball. A real *scorcher* of a baseball!

The Omniverse model provides a structure that will help explain the unknown. It should help solve some of our biggest problems and dilemmas regarding how gravity and repulsion affect dark matter and dark energy. We now know that dark energy may have an external source. Repulsion and gravity may engage in an information exchange through a higher dimensional curved boundary.

If this concept indeed moves you as it did me, I hope that you will keep questioning the universe. Always question everything. I did, and this is the result: In this book, we described how a single point particle became an entire universe. That one point particle is also responsible for creating all possibilities of time and space within itself. Thus, parallel universes are born within our own universe as noted by modern science. However, there is always going to be more of the picture to discover. Science always needs to be asking more questions.

The Next Step

Let us take the Omniverse model and explore it a bit further. We are sure to come up with many more questions for every concept introduced in this book. Here are a few additional questions regarding the Omniverse model, answered with infinite possibilities.

If one point particle can exist and create our universe, who is to say that only one of these point particles exists? The source contains all of the quantum possibilities of that particle, leading us to conclude that more particles can exist. Therefore, the possibility that they exist is real. How do we know that there are only two fields of energy levels related to our universe? Will we eventually expand into another level? Again, we might not want to assume that we only have one field around the source and one around the universe. We might view the Omniverse model more like an atom with multiple electron fields. With the Omniverse, each possible energy level is the possibility of another universe. The quantum possibilities of our surroundings are infinite. There will always be something bigger if we follow a repeating fractal pattern. Therefore, we must question whether there is something bigger than the Omniverse. The possibilities are infinite.

Now that we are able to understand a multi-dimensional Omniverse with infinite possibilities, what does it mean for us? Does our mind work as though it has different levels of energy? We may find that we do experience multiple energy levels of thought patterns as we expand ourselves in thought. Even the brain is designed in such a way as to store memories in a holographic manner similar to the way the universe works. Our brains are holograms wherein our memories are encoded everywhere throughout the brain. Perceptions, feeling, thoughts, emotions, knowledge, and past events become part of a person's imprint or energy signature that is stored in the form of memories.

These holographic imprints stored in the brain are an integral part of your mind. You will understand more fully the concept of the mind if you visualize all of these holograms as energies in fields that exist outside of your brain. Brain waves do exist outside of one's head and have been measured. But what does it mean to coexist in an energy field? We are physical and have properties that are energies or fields. Is that all we are?

Humans for thousands of years have told stories of their origins that sometimes include unexplainable beings. Are there other types of life, or are we a part of something else? Today, we have knowledge of what are described as "energy beings." This is a highly controversial subject, and this book is not intended to provide data to either prove or disprove the existence of life other than that which we know of on Earth. Nevertheless, sometimes it helps to drop assumptions. This leaves us with the possibility that there is more to life than just the physical component. For example, thought appears to be a nonphysical component of human beings. We have an Omniverse of energies to explore, and what it holds for us is infinity.

So how do we know that we are the only type of life in the known universe? Do we just assume it to be so until we have observed enough extraterrestrial or extradimensional life to be statistically accurate? Science assumes so because it has no data to support otherwise. But we also have no data to prove that it is not possible. If such an assumption is dropped, then life elsewhere is possible but not yet observed.

Our current notion of life also assumes that it has to be biological, or carbon-based. Why do we assume this to be true? Just because we are biological life, we assume that is the only possible pathway for life to exist until we have enough data to overturn the assumption. On the other hand, drop the assumption and leave open the possibility until you have enough data to support either argument. We are energy beings that exist in the physical world. And we can back that claim with principles of quantum physics. As scientists and explorers, we should be observing infinite and unbiased possibilities with no assumptions.

Exploring Infinite Possibilities

Infinite possibilities suggest that we should not assume that something does not happen because we have not observed it yet. Instead, we should accept that something is possible and look for support with scientific data. Therefore, we should build a model with all possibilities. We have a balanced approach and use the data, not the assumption, to form a model with an open mind. When we see without assumptions, we see endless possibilities. We see a universe teeming with interacting energies. Therefore, we have a universe full of life. Every string plucked, every vibration from a crescendo roll on a tympani, every little swirl of energy is part of someone or something's life cycle.

Everything lives and eventually dies in our universe. These are the cycles that form our lives. Stars are born of gas clouds that mature and transform into different types of new beginnings. Some become supernovae and spread their matter outward, thus contributing to another generation of stars and solar systems. Some become black holes and begin consuming matter. Black holes grow in size and force. Supermassive black holes attract matter in such a way that galaxies form around them. Every galaxy has a supermassive black hole at its nucleus. Galaxies attract each other to form clusters. Clusters have unique structures called filaments that develop. Now we are seeing new observational data of dark matter in these filaments. These all form patterns that indicate that everything has a life cycle and a repeating pattern.

Even the universe spreads out continuously as it expands. These are life cycles. Even an original thought has a life cycle. It develops in your mind, grows, and becomes part of your knowledge base. This book is a turning point in the life cycle of one such thought.

In this book, I am describing the life cycle of a single universe in an Omniverse that is full of infinite possibilities. One nucleus or source, one point particle or pre-Big Bang singularity, and one Inflationary Big Bang make up the Omniverse. The process acts as if a single particle were ejected from a theoretical white hole and the resulting combination of rapid inflation and continual expansion occurs at the event horizon. This creates a multidimensional system in which information cannot be lost. Included in this model is every quantum possibility for the same universe to exist in all possible states. In addition, the singularity that is used to create our universe and all possible parallel universes is only one point in another quantum probability involving infinite singularities.

I feel as if the universe came to me to ask questions regarding its origin. If the universe can think, it might be just as curious as we are. This brings us to the concept of universal consciousness, which may be the sum of all forms of consciousness in the universe. Drop the assumption that this does not exist and embrace the possibility. Only observation will tell us whether it exists. Why would the universe want to know its origin? We mimic the universe with our brains. We want to know where we come from. It is endemic to our existential nature. In fact, would the universe need us to exist if it knew everything about its inception? One might say we are the universe's collective perception.

Ask yourself just two questions about your own life: How much information have you gained? How much love have you given? Now picture the universe asking the same questions. Herein lays our purpose. We do this through perception. We see, hear, taste, smell, feel, think, and perceive our surroundings. We use these perceptions in order to build a mental model of our world. As we grow in knowledge, so does our ability to perceive. We are now using technology to observe. Everything we know goes back to the collective consciousness. Thus, information is not lost.

The Independence Age of Discovery

Someday after the Omniverse model has been thoroughly studied, we may find that the Omniverse described in this book is just the beginning to a new era of science with new discoveries about the universe and beyond. Since this model describes one source object with one point particle in a field, it is similar to a hydrogen atom. The atom has a single electron in a field around a nucleus consisting of one proton and one neutron. Chemists discovered and classified atoms to build the periodic table. Someday, we may have the same for multiple Omniverse "atoms" categorized according to the amount of multiple point particles. We may find bonds between atoms and lattices upon which the bonds are forged. Of course, being a geologist, I would want to envision the bigger picture of the Omniverse model as a crystal lattice.

It sounds like I am following my own pattern of guidance. While I am not attempting to explain all of the energies or phenomena in our universe, I have found that the possibilities related to our existence are infinite yet explainable. It is a great pleasure for me to see that this started from such a simple idea many years ago, and that the Omniverse model has seemed to fit with every great scientific achievement and discovery. Every observation and every discovery has helped me piece the big picture together over the last two decades. As far as science has taken us to this day, I still view it as an infant. In our infancy, we have not experienced all that the universe has to offer.

One thing for sure is that humanity will never stop discovering. Our nature is to question and to experience all things. The Omniverse is telling us the universe's secrets. With science in its infancy, we are opening our eyes and awakening for the very first time. This is our Independence Age of discovery. Welcome to your Universe! You are free to explore.

ABOUT THE AUTHOR

David Bertolacci is a Professional Geologist. He studied geology with emphasis on crystallography and geochemistry in 1992 and earned a Master's Degree in 2009 in environmental science. Geology and environmental science were just a stepping stone on the path to knowledge about our universe. Mr. Bertolacci has always asked the question regarding the how the creation of the universe unfolded.

He has gained knowledge of the universe for nearly two decades by studying astronomy, physics, material science, and spiritual concepts. His combination of logical methods with a spiritual approach led to the scientific proposal of the Grand Slam Theory of the Omniverse. When this work was set forth, he believed we could make the Omniverse model into a reality. With this book, he hopes to achieve this goal.

Website: www.GrandSlamTheory.com

Facebook Omniverse page: www.facebook.com/GrandSlamTheory

REFERENCES

1. Hawking, Steven, *A Brief History of Time*, Bantam Books, 1988.
2. Aristotle, *On the Heavens*, 340BC
3. Newton, Isaac, *Philosophiae Naturalis Principia Mathematica*, 1687
4. Penrose, Roger, *Cycles of Time, an Extraordinary New View of the Universe*, Borzio Book, 2010
5. Kant, Immanuel, *Critique of Pure Reason*, 1871
6. Einstein, Albert, *Relativity: The Special and General Theory*, Third Edition, 1920
7. Guth, Alan, *Inflationary Universe*, Perseus Books, 1997
8. Hawking, Steven and Mlodinow, Leonard, *The Grand Design*, Bantam Books, 2010
9. Amendola, Luca and Tsujikawa, Shinji, *Dark Energy, Theory and Observations*, Cambridge University Press, 2010
10. Kaku, Michio, *Parallel Worlds, A Journey through Creation, Higher Dimensions, and the Future of the Cosmos*, Anchor Books, A Division of Random House, Inc., 2005
11. Planck, Max, *Quantum Hypothesis*, 1900
12. Kaku, Michio, *Quantum Field Theory, a Modern Introduction*, Oxford University Press, Inc., 1993
13. Randall, Lisa, *Higgs Discovery, the Power of Empty Space*, First Ecco Solo Edition, HarperCollins e-books, 2012

14. Susskind, Leonard and Lindesay, James, *An Introduction to Black Holes, Information, and the String Theory Revolution, The Holographic Universe*, World Scientific Publishing Co. Pte. Ltd., 2005

15. Kaku, Michio, *Introduction to Superstrings and M-Theory*, Second Edition, Springer-Verlag New York, Inc., 1999

16. Randall, Lisa, *Warped Passages, Unraveling the Mysteries of the Universe's Hidden Dimensions*, First Harper Perennial edition, HarperCollins Publishers, 2006

17. Kaku, Michio, *Physics of the Impossible, A Scientific Exploration Into the World of Phasers, Force Fields, Teleportation, and Time Travel*, Anchor Books, A Division of Random House, Inc., 2008

18. Talbot, Michael, *The Holographic Universe*, HarperCollins Publishers, 1991, Reissued in 2011

19. Razieh Pourhasan, Niayesh Afshordi, and Robert B. Mann, *Out of the White Hole: A Holographic Origin for the Big Bang*, (http://arxiv.org/pdf/1309.1487v1.pdf, accessed September 21, 2013)

RESOURCES

Here are some organizations you may be interested in:

Comfy Soul
Offers life coaching services and comes highly
recommended by all of our friends!
www.comfysoul.com

The Art of Living
Provides classes and talks for developing one's
meditation techniques and practicing.
www.artofliving.org

Hay House
Provides publishing services for books by spiritual
and scientific authors.
www.hayhouse.com

Agape International Spiritual Center
Home of Reverend Michael Bernard Beckwith, this is a
transdenominational gathering of greatness!
www.agapelive.com